BEAUTIFYING REJECTION: THE GREAT EXCHANGE

BIANCA BROWN

Copyright © 2023 BIANCA BROWN

All rights reserved.

ISBN: 979-8-218-35146-5

No part of this publication may be reproduced, stored in a retrieval system, or transmitted in any form or by any means- electronic, mechanical, photocopy, recording, or otherwise without written permission from the author. Email contact: www.iambiancabrown.com

Cover Design by Bianca Brown
www.iambiancabrown.com

Editing by A.T. Destiny Awaits Group LLC
atdestinyawaitsgroup@gmail.com

BEAUTIFYING REJECTION: THE GREAT EXCHANGE

Scripture quotations marked (AMP) are taken from the Amplified Bible, Copyright © 2015 by The Lockman Foundation. Used by permission.

Scripture quotations marked (ASV) are public domain in the United States.

Scripture quotations marked (BSB) The Berean Bible and Majority Bible texts are officially dedicated to the public domain as of April 30, 2023. All uses are freely permitted.

"Scripture quotations marked (ESV) are from The ESV® Bible (The Holy Bible, English Standard Version®), © 2001 by Crossway, a publishing ministry of Good News Publishers. Used by permission. All rights reserved."

Scripture quotations marked (KJV) are public domain in the United States.

"Scripture quotations marked NAS or NASB taken from the (NASB®) New American Standard Bible®, Copyright © 1960, 1971, 1977, 1995, 2020 by The Lockman Foundation. Used by permission. All rights reserved. lockman.org"

Scripture quotations marked (NIV) are taken from the Holy Bible, New International Version®, NIV®. Copyright © 1973, 1978, 1984, 2011 by Biblica, Inc.™ Used by permission of Zondervan. All rights reserved worldwide. www.zondervan.com The "NIV" and "New International Version" are trademarks registered in the United States Patent and Trademark Office by Biblica, Inc.™

Scriptures marked NKJV are from the New King James Version®. Copyright © 1982 by Thomas Nelson. Used by permission. All rights reserved.

Scripture quotations marked (NLT) are taken from the *Holy Bible*, New Living Translation, copyright ©1996, 2004, 2015 by Tyndale House Foundation. Used by permission of Tyndale House Publishers, Carol Stream, Illinois 60188. All rights reserved.

Scripture quotations marked TPT are from The Passion Translation®. Copyright © 2017, 2018, 2020 by Passion & Fire Ministries, Inc. Used by permission. All rights reserved. ThePassionTranslation.com.

BEAUTIFYING REJECTION: THE GREAT EXCHANGE

CONTENTS

	Foreword	1
	Dedication & Acknowledgments	7
	Introduction	15
1	An Inconceivable Gift	22
2	A Wandering Soul	36
3	The Entry of Rejection	50
4	How Rejection Affects Us	54
5	How to reject - Rejection (A TOOL)	60
6	Breaking Free from Fantasies: Aligning the Heart with Heavenly Truth	65
7	Breaking Through Numbness: God's Call To Emotional Clarity	73
8	The Wake Up Call: Accepting The Divine Plan Over Popularity	81
9	Own Your Ashes: Preparing for a Divine Exchange	91
10	Dismantling Disaster: Making Way For God's Newness	101
11	Interlude: Let's Take A Break	106

12	Divine Sufficiency: Living In God's Abundance	109
13	Heart's Eclipse: The Shadow of Self-Condemnation	120
14	Nourishing the Heart: Cultivating Your Inner Sanctuary	124
15	Breathing Life: The Thoughts That Sustain Our Hearts	131
16	Shedding the Victim's Cloak: Embracing Divine Empowerment	138
17	More Than Meets the Eye: Rethinking the Role of Beauty	151
18	Knowing your value	159
19	Fortifying the New You: Resisting Life's Contradictions	163
20	From Residue to Restoration: Believing in the Remnants	170
21	Borrowed belief	180
22	From False Foundations to Solid Ground: The Journey from Misplaced to Anchored Confidence	192
23	The Lavish Life Redefined	205
24	Reflect, Not Rebuke: Escaping the Trap of Judgment	225
25	Crafted by the Divine: Living as God's Idea	242

BEAUTIFYING REJECTION: THE GREAT EXCHANGE

Foreword

It was the Spring of 2022. The bitterly cold winter had just ended. The birds were singing again, trees were budding, flowers were blooming, and the grass was green. Spring had sprung! The sky was blue, and there was a sweet smell in the air.

Everything around me was calm and beautiful. But inside of me, I was perplexed and restless. A heavy burden I could not explain had come upon my soul.

I decided to go and pray on a prayer mountain (where I often resort for prayer and meditation) to seek the face of the Lord. I got to the mountain at about 8:30 pm that fateful night.

There, on the prayer mountain, I poured out my heart to the Lord. So deep was the agony of my soul I could not express it in words and in my understanding. So, I prayed and groaned in the spirit. For about thirty minutes, I prayed in tongues, and I prayed in the spirit. I sang in tongues, and I sang in the spirit. I poured out my heart to the Lord.

After the moment of intimacy with the Holy Spirit through prayer, worship, and intercession, I felt relieved. The burden was lifted, and my soul rejoiced. Hallelujah.

I was walking back to my car to drive down the mountain and head home when a pretty young lady walked up to me and said, "Man of God, you blessed me tonight. I have listened to you pray the whole time. Thank you for being a blessing to me. I usually go to the back of the mountain to pray. But today the Lord instructed me to wait in my car." Those were her exact words.

First, how did she know I am a pastor? Because at that point, I had never met her. I was a total stranger! Secondly, how did she know what I was praying about for her to be blessed by listening to me pray? I did not pray in English or any other languages that I speak. I spoke the language of the spirit the whole time. And she understood it!

BEAUTIFYING REJECTION: THE GREAT EXCHANGE

The only logical explanation would be she was connected in the spirit. She was on the same spiritual wavelength I was operating on that night. So she was able to connect.

That young lady is Bianca Brown, the author of this book: "BEAUTIFYING REJECTION: THE GREAT EXCHANGE."

Humanly speaking, there is nothing beautiful about rejection! Beauty and rejection are almost antithetical. They are two parallels that cannot meet.

One of the hardest situations to deal with in life is rejection. Why? Because it is not of your making. It is what others did to you. You have little or no control over that.

But in this book, "Beautifying Rejection: The Great Exchange," Bianca will show you that it is possible to make something beautiful out of your ugly past. That you can give the pieces of your broken past to the

Lord and He will put them back together again. That includes rejection.

The author has proven in this book that we can trade all the negative side effects of rejection, which include but are not limited to, hurt feelings, shame, loneliness, bitterness, embarrassments, depression, social anxiety, and rage, for self-acceptance, joy, peace, calmness, godliness, contentment, and a life of productivity.

The word rejection resonates with many of us and our experiences in life. Even our Lord and Savior, during His sojourn here on earth, did not escape its bite.

John 1:11 says:

"He came to his own people, and even they rejected him." (New Living Translation)

What you will see in this book as you glean through its pages is nothing but a true account of a woman who had been to hell and back! But with God on her side, and her own determination and resilience, has been able to reject rejection and embrace all the beauties heaven has bestowed on her. She has made herself vulnerable to expose the lies of the enemy.

We've all had our own share of difficulties and challenges in life. But do not allow any of those difficulties and challenges to derail you from your passion and God's purpose for your life. Instead, continue to develop yourself in your giftings and calling. Devote yourself to seeking the Lord. Invest in self-development. You are already on your way to freedom by reading this book!

The content of this book provides an escape route for those who have been trapped by long years of abuse, maltreated by trusted friends, exploited by exes, and rejected by society.

Bianca has written this book in a lucid literary style. Which is my favorite style of writing. This style of writing is easy to read. It takes away all the ambiguities and presents a clear understanding to the reader.

It is my prayer and sincere desire that as you read through this book, the light of the Lord will shine on your spirit. That you will be set free and find freedom from every chain that holds you bound. The Spirit of the Lord will illuminate your spirit and set your heart on fire so you can run with passion and precision to fulfill all your God-given potentials.

Now the table is set! Come ye who are hungry and thirsty; come ye who have been molested, ridiculed, wrongfully accused, rejected. Come, drink from the river of life offered to you through this book. Drink and find rest for your soul.

Happy Reading!!

Tim Thompson, *Lead Pastor*
Living Hope International Christian center
811 West Jefferson Street, Grand Prairie Tx, 75051

Dedication & Acknowledgements

There would be no book if it weren't for the love and support of the spiritual giants who walk with me through the many ups and downs of my life.

To my dear sweet Kenneth, currently my only child: you have inspired Mommy more than you know. The joy that I have watching you grow and evolve into the teenager you are becoming is a gift from God that I never knew I needed. Your very existence has challenged me to fight for you when I hadn't even learned how to fight for myself. I admire your strength, your joy, your innocence, your creativity, and your heart. I pray that I evolve even more into the mom you need so that you will become even more of the Man of God you are called to be! I love you, sweetheart!

I have to start this space with thanks and gratitude to the woman who gave me life, my mother Clarissa Brown, to whom I dedicate this book. Even though my mother is no longer here with me, I cherish the memories and lessons that live on. She was a woman full of love, joy, optimism, and the person who gave me my creative eye. Even while she lived, I didn't feel that she always received her just due in life, but I pray that I am a part of the generation that walks fully into the promises of God to honor the sacrifices of my mother.

Three women who aren't far behind, if not right beside my mother in playing vital roles in my life are my Grandmother Rosa Brown, my aunt Sheryl Brown, and my Aunt (Second grandmother) Lorena Littlejohn (I pretty much had two Moms and two grandmothers growing up lol). These three women are the reason why I can never say that I've had a hard life because no matter how cold the world was, they always embraced and supported me. I say to them personally, thank you for never turning your back on me in my many dark days. Thank you for being the one to teach me how to pray and establish my relationship with God. Thank you for showing me the kind of love and support that only a privileged group of humans get to experience. Thank you for sacrificing for me to live out my purpose even in the moments when you were fighting to live out your own. Thank you for shutting down the judgments of others about my situation even when I myself gave you no glimmer of hope. Thank you for seeing more in me when I didn't want to live another day. I don't know what is coming completely but I know that my promise to you is that your sacrifice and seeds into me will yield more than we can even imagine. I can't wait to materialize all that God has shown me to bless you and I pray that I honor my family name and make you proud.

To my Uncle/Cousin Abraham (everyone in my family takes on multiple roles) thank you for being a role model to not just me but my son as well. Thank you for giving me advice even when I was hard-headed but being protective enough to never quit advising me until I got the point. You are a father figure to many, but I thank you for including me in the fold of those you teach and protect when you never had to.

To my grandfather Clarence Brown, my "PAW PAW", the only man who can ever call me by the nickname "BB"; we didn't get to spend many years together but the years we did spend meant so much to me. Grandpa, I appreciate and love you for always treating me like your little princess. It was evident that I held a sacred space in your heart and even though you are no longer here, that will never stop you from holding a space in my heart too.

To James Clark, the man who has become a key pillar in my life and someone whom I can confide in: I want to say thank you for being a man of integrity and showing up as a trustworthy person to whom I can bare the parts of my story that I rarely share with anyone. Thank you for loving me beyond my gifts and loving me for just who I am at the core. Thank you for the honor you have given me of not just being in your life but also being in Duke and Deacon's life. The joy of being around you all and the support that you have brought into my life has helped me to bring this book into this world.

BEAUTIFYING REJECTION: THE GREAT EXCHANGE

There are a host of mentors who played a role in my becoming whom I would not dare to leave out of this list of appreciation.

Lawanda Grant you were, and still are, one of the strongest and most vibrant women I know. You were the first person to hand me a mic to speak before I even knew I had something to say. Thank you for showing a little quiet girl how to shake off life, work for God, love God's people, and walk in grace and dignity no matter what.

DeKhari Liehl you know that I can say so much about you and get all mushy. Out of the many people who have taught me, you are one of the people that have labored with me the most, activated me in the prophetic, and challenged me at all times to stop being passive and think critically. I received some hard lessons that called me higher and matured me spiritually in ways that I never knew were possible. I am grateful for everything that you have poured into me even at the expense of having time and space to yourself. I was very over the top sometimes but thank you for always giving me grace and being patient with me.

Dr. Marie Sesay, you are incredible! Thank you for giving an ill-prepared college student an opportunity to glean from a scholar and executive such as yourself. You were the first of your kind that I had ever seen break glass ceilings in education by becoming the only black-woman at Lone Star College to hold the office of a Dean, at the time of me being a student. I learned so much from you and I appreciate the time and opportunity given. I will always look up to you and carry the lessons you gave me throughout my life.

Shari Robinson, I couldn't leave you out. I spent a lot of time working with you and you taught me a lot professionally but even more about being peaceful in the way that I interacted with others. Before meeting you, I always thought my soft voice was a con, but you taught me that it was a plus in my daily life. Thank you for showing me how to fully embrace the softer side of who I am.

Evangelist Latonya Otems, I would have never known that as I walked the college hallways I would run into a mighty woman of God such as yourself. You are a powerful Evangelist that flows strategically in the prophetic, a prayer warrior, a business Mogul, and a fashionista. I learned so much from you and I truly value our time together.

Dr. Shamieka Dean, you played a major role in my elevation into business and learning even more about the prophetic. Without me ever asking, thank you for allowing me to operate on assignments I never knew I could and work in capacities that I never knew existed in me. You shared my name and you gave me a place to birth creativity. Thank you for the session and courses that helped me birth this book. I honor you as the powerhouse you are!

Tiffany Amanetu, words can't describe my gratitude for your guidance and insightful advice. You labored with me for years and truly believed in what God was doing in my life. People like you don't come around every day and I appreciate your heart of Gold!

To Minister Barbara Macon, thank you for your obedience! The prophecy God sent through you has put me on a life-long journey that I could have never dreamed of! I honor you!

INTRODUCTION

*The thief comes only to steal and kill and destroy; I
came that they may
have life, and have it abundantly.
John 10:10*

The first thing to be known and remembered as you walk through this journey of healing, self-discovery, illumination, and becoming your Godly-best self is:

You have the right to light up a room.
   You have the right to feel and be confident.
   You have the right to love yourself as a person.
   You have the right to feel and be beautiful.
   You have the right to live in your full potential.
   You have the right to be a whole and happy human being.
   You have the right to feel special.
   You have the right to have a life worth living.

Now, I know that it's a little unorthodox to start a book in this manner, but I'm sure that if you are reading this, you are out of the box yourself (which is your signature of approval from God)! The very purpose of this book is to take you on a journey of self-discovery through the process of God-discovery. The road to your best self is by way of meeting the God who has already paved the way to a life of fullness, free of the limiting beliefs you once held about yourself and who you truly are.

Did you know that God loves your quirks? Did you know that God doesn't just love you, but he also likes you?

If you said "yes", then you're on the right track, and if you didn't say "Yes," then don't feel alone as most of my life I have felt the same way too. I knew God loved me as He loved everyone, but the hard part of that for me was knowing "why". I mean, what would make such a holy God love someone like me who had been pregnant at a young age, divorced, a single parent, insecure, socially awkward, horribly unstable, and ultimately rejected by life?

The answer I discovered was a groundbreaking revelation in my journey.

BEAUTIFYING REJECTION: THE GREAT EXCHANGE

So, God created man in His own image; in the image
of God He created him; male and female
He created them.
Genesis 1:27 NIV

When God looks at man, He does not look at us with a heart of judgment. He sees us as His creation and in the image of Himself. He is not looking at us to see if we are on trend; He's looking at us to count the number of hairs on our head because that's just how much He adores us. We are the only entity on this planet that has the privilege of being made in His image and likeness. Think about it, out of over 8 million living species on the earth; God chose to make us a part of the one species with his image and likeness. Just the fact alone that we have been sat in this class should make us feel special and chosen because that means that God cherished our souls before we could even do anything to earn or disqualify ourselves from His love.

The truth is that when God looks at us, He doesn't classify us as worthy or unworthy by our circumstances because those change, and contrary to popular belief, God loves to use what we perceive as a mess to create a beautiful picture! In fact, the blessing of salvation and acknowledging God as our creator is that God does not need our human proclivities or piety to deem us worthy because worthiness was paid for by the sacrifice of Jesus on the cross. After a long healing journey, I have come to realize that the rejection, self-doubt, self-hatred, and depression I had for years were not a reflection of how God felt about me.

God never thought that I was ugly; he only saw beauty (Yep, the kids on the playground weren't telling the truth).

God didn't think I was useless; as a matter of fact, He had a great plan for my life (I guess my high school grades lied too)!

The rejection from others and thoughts of self-hatred were all lies and accusations from the enemy! They were just a false by-product of core beliefs that I had been conditioned to believe about myself for most of my life, core beliefs that held me up from living the great life that God had promised his children would live.

BEAUTIFYING REJECTION: THE GREAT EXCHANGE

After realizing this, I was ready to be free, but I didn't know how? My next thought was:

"Well, how do I overcome the lie that I'm not good enough?" "How do I stop believing something I have believed for years?" "How do I begin to walk in the confidence of God?"

These questions and revelations took me on a journey of facing the weights of past rejections that had held me back from walking in my full potential and on a constant mission of renewing my mind. Sometimes it was an ugly and painful journey, full of tears, but the ugliness of my pain led me to discover what true beauty looks like.

With all that I have gone through surrounding rejection (and it has been a lot), I won't say that I have completely obtained the fullness of my potential, which I have come to find to be the most wonderful and exciting thing about this journey of becoming. The place of "becoming" gives you the permission to explore and get to know your God-given identity and simultaneously the grace to take it one step at a time and be patient with your process.

My journey has been challenging, and because of that, it has been rewarding, leading me to greater heights in all areas of my life. I didn't write this book as a memoir of my experiences with rejection, yet God prompted me to write and share this as a blueprint for others to discover what I call "the beautified" you! God told me, "I need you to share your story," not because of fame but because He had YOU in mind when He allowed me to go through the process (yes, you who are reading this right now…he counted you in my friend).

What I'm getting at here is that there is a beautiful and illuminating you just on the other side of your choice to walk through a journey of healing from rejection. Honestly, I don't want you just to read this book as inspiration, but I hope you will accept the challenge of going through your very own tailor-made process to discover your greatness. Sometimes it will be challenging, and sometimes it will feel invasive, but the promise here is that it will be liberating.

I know that it's not easy, but I believe you have read to this point because you are ready to be free and fill the space in our world that you were created to fill. Embark on this journey with me, and I will hold your hand as your God Sister because it's time for you to Shine...Quirks and all!

> *"Arise, shine; for your light has come, And the glory of the LORD has risen upon you."*
> *Isaiah 60:1ESV*

1

An Inconceivable Gift

Beautifying rejection is not just about a change of appearance; It is a sanctification process to be beautified by God.

    It's a cleansing,
        It's a washing,
             It's a renewal.

    Towards the end of 2017, God began to speak to me very heavily about beauty. This was during my college season, and I was bright-eyed and excited about my future. At that time, I felt like I had applied myself during college and that I was headed for greatness, so (pridefully) I could see why God was speaking to me about beautifying my life. However, I was unprepared for the rude and cruel reality that would hit me shortly after graduation, making the beginning of 2018 a tough season for me. Here I was, an honor graduate with no prospects, broke, illness stricken, with rejection letters flooding in.

This time of my life felt so embarrassing and discouraging. I remembered what God said and wondered how He could speak to me about beauty yet lead me into such an ugly place.

Here I was looking for a job; I searched high, low, and everywhere in between, and yet doors kept closing. If that wasn't enough, I was getting sick, and doctors couldn't find out what was wrong with me.

I remember the 2 a.m. moments crying out to God with tears streaming down my face, saying, "Where is the beauty you promised me?" I was financially broke and broken in my heart. Even worst, looking for a job while battling depression just makes finding an opportunity that much harder because depression is a stench that repels creative opportunities.

While in this season, the only thing that I could say to keep myself above the swallowing hole of disappointment was, "Don't stop moving." Sometimes the only defense you have against the depression chasing you is to just keep moving.

So, I ended up putting the skills that I had to work as a volunteer or inside gigs. I did many things, including make-up, Photography, and even Design.

I was micro-marketing my skills, all while I waited for a corporate job to come through. Soon after, I started getting a few gigs, little makeup here and photography there, and I even got a big opportunity to do some design work for someone who had a television show. My current branding business wasn't even formed yet and was only an intuitive dream. Even though I had a few gigs I still had no direction.

Here I was, with all of these different skills, and I didn't know how to put them together, use them, and what I needed them for. I had no clear vision.

The season was so tough that I knew if I didn't connect with others who were headed in the right direction, I would soon lose my battle with depression. In this space, I decided to set up a session with an industry leader named Dr. Shamieka Dean. Here I was with unstructured talent, and I was sitting in this meeting over the phone, sharing all my skills and obstacles. Suddenly, Dr. Dean says, "Beautifying rejection," and she says, "Seek the Lord about what that means for you." I was struck because instantly Holy Spirit brought back to my remembrance what He had been speaking to me about beauty the year prior.

Not only that, but it confirmed a word that I received three weeks before we met.

One Sunday, during a visit to a local church that I would visit from time to time in Houston, called New Jerusalem, I was singled out in the back of the church while walking in the hallway. A lady named Barbara Macon, sitting in a chair, looked at me and said in an instant, "You are pretty now, but God is going to beautify you. He is going to beautify your life and make it as beautiful as the dress you have on". Again, I was rendered speechless. The dress that I was wearing was blue, pink, yellow, and white with all different types of flowers on it. I received the word that she spoke that day.

Throughout this season, God continued to illuminate the word beauty everywhere I went. I began to seek him deeper and realized that what God was saying was beyond the vanity of how we usually refer to beauty, and I wanted to get a better understanding.

> *to bestow on them a crown of beauty*
> *instead of ashes, the oil of joy*
> *instead of mourning, and a garment of praise*
> *instead of a spirit of despair.*
> *Isaiah 61:3*

Immediately I was taken to Isaiah 61:3, a scripture I had seen many times before. However, this time when I looked at the word beauty, I didn't just want to read it; I wanted to inhale it as the living word of the Lord for my life!

I was at my breaking point and done with the mediocre knowledge of my mind. I needed my heart to understand what God meant when He said that He would give me beauty for ashes. It sounded great, but I began to ask God questions like:

- How can you beautify the places in me that are depressed? How can you beautify the spaces that still feel rejected?
- How can you beautify me when I don't feel like I'm good enough?
- What was the beauty that God had for a person like me who never felt that they were a part of what beauty was?
- How could I obtain it from him?
- What did I have to do to give him the ashes?
- How do you lay ashes down after carrying them for a lifetime? How could I even define what ashes truly were?

An Inconceivable gift

It was so inconceivable how a person could go all of their life in the seat of rejection, feeling like they were never good enough, not gracious enough, not classy enough, and suddenly, one day, God could make them beautiful.

> *"For my thoughts are not your thoughts, neither are your ways my ways, declares the LORD. "As the heavens are higher than the earth, so are my ways higher than your ways and my thoughts than your thoughts.*
> *Isaiah 55:8-9 NIV*

I finally came to a conclusion where I realized that my analysis of God's promise to give me beauty wouldn't yield anything but more questions that would send me on an endless journey of distraction.

Oftentimes, if the enemy can't stop us from seeking God, he will send us on a mission of distraction to slow us down and wear us out. These distractions can come in the form of valid reasons, questions, and excuses. The key to recognizing that it's the enemy at play is by deciphering where the valid reason, question, or excuse is leading you too after you engage it.

The enemies' plots will always lead us back to self and worldly desires because these plots are created to engage us in the cares of this world instead of the cares of the Lord.

The questions that had kept me constantly walking in circles in my mind and never getting to the place of completion were similar to the children of Israel after God had delivered them from Egypt. A trip that should have taken 11 days took 40 years.

The story of the children of Israel has always been so interesting because I could understand how a group of people could wander around without God, but not how a group of people could wander around in the wilderness WITH God? (Well, my journey has led me to a place where I understand what it means to wander around in a desert, even knowing the Father of the Universe.)

I always thought to myself that it would be okay if I were wandering and walking around in circles without God because at least I would know why I hadn't made it yet because I was obviously wandering around without the God of everything. However, it's a whole other thing to pass the same spot over and over with God on my side. It's another thing to walk in circles when you have God's promise, favor, and backing but you don't have God's fruit yet and you feel stuck.

The Children of Israel walked around and around because of their complaining, disobedience, and double mindedness towards God until God said that due to this, He would not allow the generation who was delivered from Eygpt to see the promised land. So, He allowed them to go around for 40 years until those who were disobedient and double-minded died. Per my calculation, they must have passed the pathway to their promise at least 1,327 times, but every time they got there to the place of their deliverance, their habitual attitude towards God, their questions, and their complaining just started a new cycle of wandering and another wilderness experience.

If there is anything that this teaches us is that God will deliver you with your old mindset, but he will not allow you to walk into the promised land with it. Not just that, but He will also walk with you through an ongoing wilderness until the disobedience and murmuring of the flesh dies.

In my season of hardship, I realized that God is very patient, and he does not live in time, but we do, and I surely didn't want to spend 40 years going around the same mountain of questions. However, I needed to know how to move beyond the strong emotions and feelings connected to rejection.

God showed me that the only way I could win this kind of fight was instead of asking endless questions, I had to surrender my belief system to God and focus on his glory instead of my confusion. This choice and positioning will unlock the process that is beautification. As we surrender our ideals and trust God, we unlock His ability to work as He wills in our life.

I began this process by seeking God and looking for the transformation power in Him, being willing to tackle what the beautification process really was. It was a choice that would lead me into a divine moment where I would encounter God, beautifying the rejection that had plagued me my whole life.

The depth of beautifying rejection is exchanging the *reflection of self* for the *reflection of God*, no longer looking in the mirror and seeing our past hurts, our frustrations, or our measures of worthiness according to this fallen world. It's about finally looking in the mirror to see what God sees about us and about his Kingdom children. However, this is a process that must happen from the perspective of God with total abandonment of what we have ever known about ourselves and life. Forgiving and letting go of our yesteryear for our today and future.

What I've come to discover is that we forgive our bullies more easily than we let go of their accusations. Furthermore, we forgive our bullies more than we forgive ourselves for making mistakes which cause us never to allow ourselves to move on and live life. Anytime we stay in the place of rejection, we chain ourselves to a path of seeking validation to scratch the itching desire to belong.

Rejection makes us thirsty for validation and approval from others, but God wants to satisfy our thirst with a beautiful stream located in us that never runs dry of His Glory. The time has come for us to meet at the crossroad with God, where he unlocks the beauty of His presence within us, like the Woman at the well to whom God gave living water.

However, this can only be so when we sit at the master's feet with our ashes— and when I say sit at his feet, I don't mean in the noise of what sounds like worship but sometimes in the silence and stillness.

Silence the noise

I will admit that one of the hardest things for me to do has been to sit with God, without music, preaching, and speaking in tongues, but just to sit and be in the sweet rest of His presence. Through my research, I soon realized that this is generally an issue for those with abandonment and rejection issues. These traumas' residuals often result in an "orphan spirit." An Orphan Spirit can be defined in various ways, but I will say that it is a stronghold on the mindset of someone who has experience rejection and abandonment on a very deep level. One of the ways an orphan spirit manifests is by causing a person to think that they must earn the love of others. However, this alone causes other issues like a ripple effect throughout our lives, such as:

- Cause us to look for praise from others as a form of validation
- Do things outside of the character of God to gain a sense of belonging
- Push people away due to jealousy and insecurity
- Feel like a forever outsider and Black sheep even in great relationships

And so much more...

Since many of us have experienced rejection and, as a result, have been singled out, ostracized, or even abandoned, it tends to be the position we assume. As for me, whenever I would meet someone new or hang out with someone, I would just assume the mindset of not being qualified or unwanted in a space. So, when it was time to sit in the presence of God, I would assume the same position. This made sitting in the stillness a battle and frustrating ordeal, constantly overanalyzing if God was pleased with me or not and if He even liked me. At least when I was busy in God's presence, I felt that I was in control and earning His affection. Busyness in his presence also kept me from the blistering silence that felt like His rejection. So, when I knew I needed to settle down in His presence, I would get busier because I saw myself as unworthy and could not bear another rejection.

I began avoiding my quiet time with God because sitting felt so isolating. Every time I sat with Him, I would have to confront all the tormenting thoughts of what I wasn't doing right and, even worse, images of who around me seemed perfect. So, I was good with Church and the hallelujah scream, but every time God tugged on me and said, "Come away with me," it felt like a punishment.

My life experiences and my messed-up view of myself had turned what should have been sacred into a chore. I have learned that when we don't see ourselves as God sees us, then sitting with the Father can become a chore instead of a pleasure.

Turning our relationship with God into a chore is the enemy's strategy to cause us to revoke our own access to the power in God's presence. Not having the mental access to the presence of the Lord is the enemy's plot to cause our lives to spiral into the depths of insecurity, confusion, and depression. The enemy knows that without access to the Lord's presence, we cannot have the promises and breakthrough that come along with it. The Bible says in the presence of the Lord, there is fullness of joy (Psalm 16:11), and Nehemiah 8:10 teaches that the joy of the Lord is our strength. Without God's presence, we lose our ability to be able to live a life of value, a life of excitement, and a life of joy. God's presence is the oxygen we need to be made whole. I have shared this with you because I want you to recognize the enemy's scheme and then choose to jump over the hurdles and lies. So even through this process, allow yourself to get still and quiet in His presence. Pray this prayer anytime you need help:

BEAUTIFYING REJECTION: THE GREAT EXCHANGE

Prayer: Dear God, forgive me when I felt that I could not come to you and sit with you. I admit that I am struggling within myself, but I ask that you help me to see myself as you see me. Thank you for choosing me when I wasn't even aware of You. Thank you that I am fully loved before I make an action. Help me to have a relationship with you that is built on love and acceptance, not the need to earn your affection. I ask that you help me to know in my heart that silence is not a sign of rejection but a mark of your love that I can rest in you. Guide me through this journey as only you can. In the name of Jesus. Amen

2

A Wandering Soul

Am I fat? Am I too quiet? Do you think I should cut my hair, get extensions, or maybe wear my hair natural? Do you think that I can really sing? Do you like me?

I believe the only thing more frustrating than being rejected is not knowing the "why" behind it.

These were questions that I would constantly ask my peers throughout grade school, hoping that one day I would find an answer as to why I wasn't accepted by the "IN" crowd and receive some clues as to how I could finally fix myself to be the size, depth, and volume that was required to fit in. I surely thought at that age that maybe a simple diet, braces, acne cream, and long hair extensions better known as "a weave," could get me there.

I always felt very misunderstood, overlooked, and never chosen.

The pain of rejection from my peers was a common theme from as far back as the daycare sandbox. The echo of cruel childhood nicknames constantly rang in my ear, like "fat girl," and critiques to accessorize them, such as: "dark and ugly." The songs that the kids made up to torment me arrested my mind long after the days of walking down the hallways of grade school had ended. It seemed that no matter what age I was, how accomplished I became, or how great I looked, those memories kept me burdened, depressed, and insecure.

Have you ever felt like no matter what you did, it still seemed like you could never hit the mark?

If so, I sympathize with you because I have felt like this most of my life. Through my journey of getting to know God, I have learned that another enemy tactic to derail us is introducing trauma as early in our life as he can. The enemy formulated the teasing, mockery, and insults early in life to make chosen people like me and you feel so insignificant that we never see how loved and beautiful we truly are. I call them *seeds of negative perception*; in brief, it means to saturate a heart with an inaccurate and ungodly view of self. This is something that you and I will work through by learning how to exchange our perception for God's discernment, as it will never lead you wrong.

Unfortunately, for much of my young life, I had not come into uncovering anything that could set me free from these negative perceptions. To be even more transparent, long after I learned that everything my bullies told me wasn't true, I continued to feel the pain of their words because even lies hurt too, and their impact can last a lifetime if not dealt with! Well into my adulthood, I could still vividly remember the torment of rejection while walking down the middle school hallways with my heart beating so hard and fast that I could feel its rhythm in my toes. All because I was constantly anxious about the possibility of someone cracking a joke about me, pointing, and laughing, or the girls even trying to fight or jump me.

By the time I made it to High school, being socially awkward, never accepted or respected in a society that I so longed to be a part of, felt like my lot in life. The constant search for acceptance kept me in motion as I searched for at least one corner of the earth where I belonged or could at least be tolerated! I started with the cheerleaders and quickly discovered my size disqualified me. I then tried academics, which worked until algebra broke my heart, and my teacher began to call me "that old Brown girl," eluding to my talking habit. I then tried the cool kid's crowd until they realized my shoes were knock-offs from the flea market. Next up, the very limited and only gothic group in the hood with black lipstick, studded dog collars around their neck, and notebooks with skull graphics, I quickly realized I was too happy-go lucky for them to even be seen with me.

Last stop, choir, but not even the fact that I could carry a tune and win competitions, hid the fact that I was socially awkward in discussions and not yet able to be myself because I didn't know myself. I can even remember being one of the soloists in the choir for my high school graduation as all of my family, along with at least 3000 onlookers, listened and cheered as we sang our goodbyes. After singing my part, I looked behind me, to the left and the right, as tears of my fellow classmates streamed down their faces. A mood of goodbye forever filled the air as we all knew that this would be the last time, we did anything together as a class. Filled with an overwhelming sense of comradely so strong that I could hug every person in the stadium, I worked up the courage to overlook the bullying, the fights, and the rejection to share in the sentimental displays (after all, none of that matters in the end). So, I turned around to share a moment of sentimental value with the girl directly in the choir stance just above me, only to have my optimism overshadowed by a roll of the eyes, a frown of disgust, and the coldest smirk I had ever seen. I slowly turned back around as my heart which was so filled with joy, was busted by the needle of rejection. The dismissal of my courageous efforts to share my heartfelt goodbyes left me questioning whether my tears or feelings were worth sharing with the people, God, or even myself.

Okay, so I think that sums up everyone... well not all! There was a group that I actually did seemingly (big inferences on seemingly) fit into if I was willing to do what it took!

BEAUTIFYING REJECTION: THE GREAT EXCHANGE

So, during the time of high school, the integration of social media was just taking place, and everything was new, fresh, and unknown! Myspace was king, and sites like bebo and urban chat were an infatuation for someone seeking attention for their own agenda. The perfect place for a teenage girl with low self-esteem to get all the attention she desires and also a parent's worst nightmare!

Here I was, this 16/17-year-old girl, longing to be affirmed, with a camera phone (flip to be exact) and now with a profile page on a social media site open to millions of people all over the world; awesome kids, my age and celebrities but also people that a young girl never thinks about like: child molesters, and people who are a part of Houston, TX grossly overpopulated sex trafficking trade. I started off by posting profile photos and lying about my age; within 30 minutes, I had numerous messages from people telling me all the things that a teenage girl wants to hear. Most were inappropriate, but a soul that needs a place to belong will always prioritize quantity over quality. No matter how perverted and disrespectful the online social place was, it gave me a sense of being accepted and admired.

If the grown men approaching me weren't enough, I even got approached by random solicitors to be a part of dark cohorts of the internet in exchange for financial means. In fear of my family finding out, I told one of the soliciting assistants that I was not of age (hoping they would back off), and even though she became frazzled, she still invited me and told me not to tell anyone because I would be well taken care of. I even went as far as to meet one of the solicitors and was horrified, to say the least. The only thing I could do in their presence was pray silently that God would allow me to safely make it out of their presence.

Scared straight, I began shutting down and blocked all communication. There I was, a church kid, looking for attention in all of the wrong places and with all of the wrong people. My search for a place to belong had led me down a path of violation, inflicting on me wounds that took over a decade to heal.

The sad truth is that the only thing that makes my story unique is that I am the one telling the story right now. There are many others that can identify with the course of my life. Perhaps you on the other side of this page, reading, internalizing, and digesting these words, can vividly remember instances of your past that are identical to my story. Maybe on your quest to find acceptance and love, you found yourself in the grips of rejection and violation.

You are not alone; with social media becoming the giant that it has become; more and more people have turned to social media as their confirmer of beauty and place of acceptance. Ironically, this has more than not tended to lead a wandering soul to a deeper pit of insecurity and rejection.

The purpose of telling my story is not just to air out my dirty laundry because, honestly, it's not easy to tell. I have said things in this chapter alone that no one knows up until now but me. However, the word of God says that "we are overcomers by the words of our testimony," so it's necessary to tell my story because OUR story is not a testimony and a healing agent until we tell it. My desire is to show the healing power of God by holding out my scars of rejection to let you know that you're not alone. One of my most beloved scriptures, which I just referenced, is Revelation 12:11:

> *And they have defeated him by the blood of the Lamb and by their testimony.*

BEAUTIFYING REJECTION: THE GREAT EXCHANGE

And they did not love their lives so much that they were afraid to die.
Revelations 12:10, NLT

I believe God has a great life of healing, wholeness, and beauty waiting on you and the pathway to it will require a bearing of your heart. A huge step of moving beyond your pain is not just acknowledging your symptoms but going beyond them to see and recognize what caused them in the first place:

In this moment and in moments to come, I want you to grant yourself time to examine your life. This is the place where healing starts, and your spirit comes alive. Allow yourself to feel the pain of your hurt. I have included an exercise for you to complete. Along with this exercise, I encourage your exploration, but I also challenge you to be gentle with yourself. Allow yourself to examine your life without judgment. The young child in you will need the adult in you to be a friend and not your own self-bully.

First, I want you to recite these words:

BEAUTIFYING REJECTION: THE GREAT EXCHANGE

I Grant myself this space to examine myself and see the trauma caused by rejection and violation.

Now, write out the areas of rejection in your life, whether it be from family, friends, Romantic Relationships, Education, or in your career field. You can even use some of the following questions to get you started:

When did you first notice rejection?

_____
_____
_____
_____
_____

Who initiated the rejection?

_____
_____
_____
_____
_____

From that point on, how did that change the way you viewed that person or other people?

_____
_____
_____
_____
_____

Did it alter your behavior and/or the way you interacted with people?

_____
_____
_____
_____
_____

Can you see its effects in your current life? Where?

_____
_____
_____
_____
_____

Now that you have written some of your wounds and pain, I want you to say the prayer below:

Prayer: Abba (Father, daddy), you are more than a good father. I thank you for the privilege I've been afforded to come before you and have a close relationship with you. Thank you for the Holy Spirit that led me to this place of healing. Thank you for loving me enough to get my attention and run after me while I was running from my truth. Thank you for being patient and gentle with me until I was willing to stop and commune with you. Thank you for showing me a love that is exclusive to me and my situation. Lord, I have started the journey of healing by searching for the pain of my past and viewing the damages. Daddy, I know that I alone cannot heal myself, but I know and believe that this is a job for you. I ask you to come in and clean my heart of the trauma and my memory of the psychological damage that I have suffered as a result. Daddy, I ask you to take the ashes of rejection, violation, depression, low-self-esteem, and any pain unseen and make them into a beauty used for your glory. I know that this is a process, and I ask that the Holy Spirit walk me through and strengthen me throughout the process so that I can withstand the healing process. Most of all, drench me with your love and peace in this very moment so that I am not left uncovered by what I have discovered. I put these requests before you in full faith and belief that you will answer. I stand on your word and walk in the truth that you will never leave me nor forsake me. Have your way Pappa-God. In Jesus' name. Amen.

As your big sister, I am so proud of you for walking toward your wholeness and healing. This was not easy for you, but you did it anyway. Let this be a testament in your life that you are fully capable of doing the hard things to get where God desires you to be…WHOLE! In the meantime, review the scriptures below for encouragement when you feel low…every scripture reminds you that you are not alone:

And so, we know and rely on the love God has for us.
God is love.
Whoever lives in love lives in God, and God in them.
1 John 4:16

For I know the plans I have for you," declares the LORD, "plans to prosper you and not to harm you, plans to give you hope and a future.
Jeremiah 29:11

BEAUTIFYING REJECTION: THE GREAT EXCHANGE

But you, Lord, are a compassionate and gracious God, slow to anger, abounding in love and faithfulness
Psalm 86:15

No, in all these things we are more than conquerors through him who loved us. For I am convinced that neither death nor life, neither angels nor demons, neither the present nor the future, nor any powers, neither height nor depth, nor anything else in all creation, will be able to separate us from the love of God that is in Christ Jesus our Lord.
Romans 8:37-39

3

The Entry of Rejection

All things have to start with an entryway and a door. The entry of rejection is sneaky. It seizes moments of vulnerability at tender ages of life. Rejection tends to ambush us in the place of our vulnerability where we have let down our guard and are completely ourselves. We could even be in a place around family and friends that, by every account, we are supposed to be well assured of our safety and feel no threat, yet rejection can come and intrude on our space.

I believe the enemy sends rejection to enter the most vulnerable spaces because it is a ploy for us never to experience the freedom of vulnerability, thereby causing us to close ourselves off emotionally to the possibilities of relationships. I also believe this trick is a ploy to cause us to believe that being ourselves is not enough or may be an inconvenience to others.

I can imagine that Joseph, in the bible, probably felt this way when he told his brothers about the dream that God gave him, and they became angry. God gave Joseph a dream that one day, his family would come and bow to him, signifying that he would ultimately have a position of leadership over them. After he shared the dream, they were immediately insulted, and his brothers were jealous, which led to them rejecting him and selling him off into slavery.

I hear this passage of scripture preached in various ways, where some say that Joseph was wrong for telling his family his dream and that Joseph, in immaturity, told them the dream. I've also heard it said that Joseph didn't know how to handle his gift of prophetic dreaming. Now the Gospel of Jesus is not complicated to contradict itself; however, all of these explanations could very well apply because while the Gospel is not complicated, people truly are!

I believe Joseph was immature in sharing his dream, but more importantly, I believe that He was trying just to find a space of acceptance within his family and used his dream (ineffectively) as a bonding tool. Now this is just my theory as I see myself in him and have done this a few times before as a young lady. However, as I have also shared precious information about myself with others in an effort to bond, I have learned that many of the hardest moments of rejection I've had have come through this type of bonding. Unfortunately, sometimes the enemy tries to use all of our shortcomings and moments of vulnerability (especially early on in life) as an opportunity to create a false sense of reality that lends itself to us believing that we are inefficient and unacceptable.

However, no matter where rejection entered the picture, I know that God is more than capable of closing that door. I have included a scripture for you to stand on with authority and a written prayer for you to pray in faith below:

"To the angel of the church in Philadelphia write: These are the words of him who is holy and true, who holds the key of David. What he opens no one can shut, and what he shuts no one can open.
Revelations 3:7

BEAUTIFYING REJECTION: THE GREAT EXCHANGE

Prayer: *Father, I honor you as the almighty creator of everything! You hold the keys to every area of my life, and you know the details of what I cannot understand. Father, I pray that you will close the entryways of the spirit of rejection, even the doors that I opened on my own. In Jesus' name. Amen*

4

How Rejection Affects Us

Out of all the pet peeves that I have had, the one that bothers me the most is the stigma around people who deal with rejection issues.

Society (and sometimes even the church community) can put a negative and hopeless inference about the fact that someone may have rejection issues. I can remember many days I searched, attended church, and prayed for a word that would help me to fight against rejection but instead, I would leave feeling doomed to hell.

Many of the messages that revolved around rejection tended to sound something like this, "5 reasons why the spirit of rejection is bad," but very few had remedies for a hopeful cure. I always felt that

BEAUTIFYING REJECTION: THE GREAT EXCHANGE

I was being condemned and persuaded by the reasons it was wrong instead of coached on how to untangle myself in the web of rejection. These sermons and short talks always felt like a doctor going into a patient's room and listing five reasons why their illness is terrible and then walking out without giving them an examination or prescription. Sure, that patient could have opened the door for some of these things to happen to them, like not having the proper diet or engaging in extracurricular activities that were harmful, but nevertheless, hospitals and clinics are for the ill.

Per Merriam-Webster, the title "doctor" comes from the Latin word "docēre," which means "to teach." So here is my thought, when we go to a doctor, we are going to a teacher, someone who can point the way to healing, not someone who is in a persuasive or passive mode of just stating how bad the illness is.

When I speak about rejection, many may think of it as though it was a time and space, a moment where it all happened. Others may give advice on it as though it is an isolated incident, and to be fair, it could very well stem from an isolated incident. However, more often than not, rejection incidents tend to have a way of remaining with a person long after the moment has passed. I have found that it is not just the moment of rejection that does harm, but in fact, the trauma of rejection does more damage than the actual rejection itself. While writing this book (which took years), I began to experience physical weakness and signs of illness. It started with convulsions or cramping in my hand and then subsided from there. I went to various doctors and even well-versed neurologists, but nothing was found, so I went on with my life.

On my birthday in 2018, I decided to get a pedicure to cheer myself up after another moment of crying because I felt so depressed and unseen (birthdays were always hard for me). Upon sitting in the chair and putting my feet in the water, I began to feel tingling in my toes as though my feet had fallen asleep. I was concerned, but I became even more concerned as I realized that they were not waking up even after the pedicure was over. I didn't know what was happening to me.

Over the next four years, I went from doctor to doctor, and the answer was always the same between those who just dismissed me. All the while, the tingling had turned to numbness traveling up my legs to my waist. I would get up in the morning and sometimes fall straight on the floor. After waiting on a neurologist appointment waitlist for over a year, I finally got to an amazing resident neurologist, Dr.George Bailey, who listened to me and did a full examination.

After various MRIs (that none of the other doctors would do), it was discovered that my spine had been damaged seemingly by an autoimmune illness. I was relieved that he had found the place of my pain, but now we had to find out what caused it. I was tested for everything under the sun, I even had an invasive procedure known as a spinal tap, yet nothing could be declared.

The damage was there, but the doctor could not pinpoint the inflictor. However, my body was inflicted like someone with an auto immune condition; I was told that it seemed rare and that there were others who had similar MRI'S (body scans) who didn't walk anymore. I was told that he believed my body's immune system had attacked me, and he wasn't sure if it would happen again.

After much research, I found that not even these autoimmune diagnosed patients have a contributing factor to why the body would attack itself other than the reasons of stress. Still not having answers, as I worked with my counselor while we went through my childhood trauma, I remember my counselor saying, "The issues surrounding rejection that you have experienced in life have caused you to live in a perpetual and traumatized state of fear, and all of this has been stored in your body," which can cause autoimmune issues.

At that moment, it all clicked! The reason why the doctors couldn't find anything is that the disease wasn't under a microscope; it was in my soul. The disease of trauma from rejection had shown up and damaged my spine protection sheath, causing my nerves not to communicate as effectively. I went from being able to wear 5-inch heels to tripping and staggering over my own feet at the age of 31.

The trauma of rejection is lethal if not handled accordingly, but that is why I am sharing my story with you. I cannot stand by and watch another person suffer from the effects of rejection and the stress and trauma it causes. Rejection can cause more pain than we realize if we don't deal with the points of pain. I have placed a prayer below for you to pray against the effects of rejection and a scripture for you to meditate on.

> *No weapon formed against you shall prosper, And every tongue which rises against you in judgment You shall condemn.*
> *This is the heritage of the servants of the Lord, And their righteousness is from Me,"*
> *Says the Lord*
> *Isaiah 54:17*

Prayer: *Lord, I thank you for the promise of Isaiah 54:17 and the protection of your word even against rejection. I pray that you help me live in your promise with a mind stayed on your word and not the rejection that I have experienced. I decree and declare that illness will not develop from my trauma and that divine health is my portion! In Jesus' Name. Amen.*

5

How To Reject - Rejection (A Tool)

Self-Discovery

The rabbit hole of finding oneself can be a seemingly daunting and overwhelming place to walk into. It seems like a never-ending task of trial and error, or at least that's how it felt for me. Every time I would begin walking this journey to discover myself, as all the gurus would say was the only pathway to happiness (air quotes), it felt like I would volunteer myself to a fresh glass of depression and mental taunting from thoughts that said that I was less than and that I deserved every bad thing that was happening to me.

You see, I thought self-discovery meant reaching deep within the wounds and thoughts of my being to find out what was wrong and ultimately fix my emotional dysfunction. I wanted to look into that deep dark place that whispers lies in my ears when I am about to embark upon a new journey in my career, ministry, or even in my personal life. I don't know if you have ever come into contact with this voice before, Yet, it's the voice that says, "Who do you think you are to do   "

It's the videotape that plays a video of you over and over of the time when you were rejected or did something that made you feel a little embarrassed.

It's the feeling of defeat that comes over you when you look at everyone else in your career field or your classmates, and then you look at yourself, and you say, "Why even try?"

I call it the voice/ the video/ the feelings of the bully. What many don't tell you about self-discovery is that you don't just discover yourself. You discover and come face-to-face with the bully in you too. When I discovered this truth, I did what any person would probably do, I RAN! It sounds hilarious, but my spiritual, self-discovering, hippe-self became so intimidated by the bully, and I just didn't see how facing the bully would help me.

You see, I was already in a very depressed and hurt place, and I felt like I just couldn't take another blow. Because the bully doesn't play fair, it literally kicks people when they're down and vulnerable. I didn't know how I would see who I was when it meant that I would have to face the bully within me too. Maybe you're in that place where you feel like you can't take another blow to your confidence; rest assured that God knows the weight of the pain you have endured and the areas in you that are fragile as a result of all that you have gone through. Let me use this moment to affirm to you that your father knows and cares about your well-being and wants your journey of healing from rejection to be productive.

After crying out to God time and time again, it was as if God began to reverse engineer my healing of rejection, and that is not all; he showed me how to handle the bully first by examining the lie!

Examine the Lie

"...The devil has nothing to do with the truth. There is no truth in him. It is expected of the devil to lie, for he is a liar and the father of lies..."
_John 8:44

Can I tell you a secret about the bully that you CAN share with everyone?

The bully only has one tool it uses, which is the twisting of reality. I heard someone say that the most effective lie is a lie that contains a little bit of the truth. The effective lies told by the bully in our lives contain our real-life experiences, but what the bully does is a technique of twisting reality to cause confusion and misunderstanding. His formula is:

Situation + A spin of perspective =, therefore, you are _____(lie)_____

In order to confront and overcome the bully within, we must realize that the bully is a liar. Just because the scenario or situation that you are thinking about has a piece of truth in it does not mean that it is the whole truth. When we go on a self-discovering journey, we are not doing so in an effort to adopt half-truths about ourselves, and we are doing it so we can find out the whole truth of who God says we are. Every time you begin to get thoughts that are negative about yourself, I want you to examine the thought and see if it has the formula above. You may find that the perspective you have adopted about yourself, or your situation is just false evidence appearing real.

6

Breaking Free from Fantasies: Aligning The Heart With Heavenly Truth

Casting down arguments and every high thing that exalts itself against the knowledge of God, bringing every thought into captivity to the obedience of Christ
2 Corinthians 10:5, NKJV

Somewhere in my mind, I would imagine a day and time when all the bullies, both physical and spiritual... would finally dissipate and maybe even apologize. I envisioned a day where I was invited to hangouts with the crew, and those who rejected me in grade school would accept me. Even the teachers who didn't accept me would see me graduate college with honors, and the family members who weren't too fond of me would see that I had real value. For once in my life, I would finally be accepted and deemed worthy of close relationships.

These imaginary scenarios consumed me for years, well up into my twenties. I realized that these imaginative scenarios were my broken heart's escape from the pain of rejection that I held for most of my life. My imagination was my dosage of numbing medication for the agony of rejection, so I lived from the motivation of these desires for most of my adolescence up into my adult life. These desires prompted me to chase things and people that were ultimately not fit to be in my life. I didn't live with the understanding that perhaps God had rejected them from participation in my life because when the only lens you have to view life through is rejection and shame, you will always believe that you are the issue instead of looking at the rejection as God's covering.

So, holding onto these hopes, I allowed myself to be consumed by my inner child's need for acceptance. The problem with living in a place motivated by our imagination is that we never participate in the present moment because the imagination's need for validation is never satisfied. I constantly needed affirmations from the people around me to feel like they cared about me. I can remember that even when I would meet someone new, I became awkward, somewhat quiet (I have never ever been a quiet person, it was just a defense mechanism), and even robotic, rendering responses that was a result of me overthinking about what I should or shouldn't say. Needless to say, I was never present because I was constantly trying to build a narrative of myself and life that would seem more acceptable, both internally through my imagination and externally to others through my behaviors.

After much soul-searching, my revelation was that my body was in the moment, but my mind was stuck at my past points of rejection.

Points of Rejection are the places in our past where self-assurance and our value were questioned by others. The place where the rejection can be traced and possibly where we learned we may have flaws that society or particular people deem unacceptable. These points are not exclusive, nor discrimina- tory, even in our Christian walk with other Christian brothers and sisters of the faith. I cannot tell you how many times I have sat in church and heard something like ..."If these people are not moving forward to the highest levels, then cut them off..." or even "if you can't handle xyz then I don't want you around me." At the point of rejection is where we can find mankind's intolerance of human qualities, generally because of mankind's own self-reflection of rejection towards ourselves imperfection.

Even though I had this understanding of how others' intolerance of imperfections was just an issue of self-manifesting in rela- tionships, I still couldn't understand how to get beyond these hopes of acceptance from people. My heart was hung up on the times I opened myself up to others, only to be shot down by the other party, which was followed by my imagination becoming my clinging to hope to have acceptance one day. I continued to do everything I could, hoping that I could be deemed qualified by those around me. I didn't realize that this had become a "High thing" known as an Idol in my life, causing me to waver at any moment. The Bible says...

> *"casting down arguments and every high thing that exalts itself against the knowledge of God, bringing every thought into captivity to the obedience of Christ"*
> *2 Corinthians 10:5, New King James Version*

I knew it wasn't good to live in a way where I acted from my need for validation or to even daydream about it, but I needed to understand the "why" behind it. Just telling my heart to move on from these relationships (or lack thereof) and to stop hoping/dreaming wouldn't heal me; it would just stop me from entering the areas of my heart that begged for validation and acceptance. However, I had come to a place in my life where I knew my approach to getting validation and feeling valuable in life was not healthy. The only way out of my endless desires to be accepted was not to just cast down my unhealthy thoughts/imagination, which means to resist them every time they came up. The other part of that scripture tells us what thoughts to cast down, which are the thoughts and imaginations "...that exalts itself against the knowledge of God...".

Let me make it plain. I couldn't cast down what I didn't know was against God. I thought it was God's will for me to have good friends and to be close to family members, and it is! God wants us to have valuable relationships and friendships. The Bible even advises us to show ourselves friendly. However, there are some doors that God closes on purpose because of reasons that He alone may only know. There have been many times when I didn't understand why he shut certain relationships down that I cherished deeply, and it would take years until I gathered the shattered pieces of my heart and understood the why behind God's ruling. Then there are other closed doors of rejection that I still don't understand and may never understand, but I came to realize that some things are not for us to understand but instead to trust God.

We must learn something about God's knowledge even as it pertains to rejection and realize that just because the rejection doesn't add up to us, that doesn't make God's judgment and decisions for us any less trustworthy to lean on.

There was a time in my life when I constantly ruminated (which means focusing and thining on a incident or past trauma in the mind repeatedly and often casually or slowly) on the things in life that had happened to me and imagined different outcomes because I never considered that God could have decided what was best for me. After rejection, we sometimes beat ourselves up over should've, could've, would've, or we do the opposite and become the victim blaming the other party for the disruption.

But maybe…Just maybe…No one is to blame…

To stop the endless mind replay of what happened and the constant methodical approach to trying to be accepted, I have to hit the road block of God's judgment and purpose. Sometimes God makes decisions that our minds cannot comprehend, even as it relates to relationships, and I have to become okay with that. I had to begin to see the past rejections as a mechanism of God's sweet covering and judgment as a shielding, protective agent over my life, cutting away things and people that would've depleted me instead of adding to me. So, from that truth, I would have to surrender my imagination and do what Colossians 3:2 says, "Set your minds on things above, not on earthly things."

I concluded in these moments that God's ruling was enough for me to let go of my rumination of a different outcome. I stopped looking for the faults in how others rejected and treated me and instead looked towards the Father who created both parties and rested there. No matter who or what we have lost, we still have the most important pieces of life with us and that is trust in the God who loved us enough to cut away what and who would no longer help us get to a better tomorrow.

Instead of giving you a prayer to pray, meditate on this scripture and ask God what imaginations need to be cast down and where you need to wake up where you have been asleep.

cast down arguments and every high thing that exalts itself against the knowledge of God, bringing every thought into captivity to the obedience of Christ

2 Corinthians 10:5, New King James Version

7

Breaking Through Numbness: God's Call To Emotional Clarity

One of the greatest tragedies I have witnessed is that we can live our whole life from the memory of ONE moment of disappointment. Sometimes we alter our entire personality and way of living because of someone's opinion of us that has no factual bases, nor does it have any ability to alter our blessing or destiny. Rejection is a very normal part of life, even though it doesn't feel like it because, at the moment, it makes you feel like you're the only one experiencing it and that no one could ever understand or relate to the way that you have been hurt. This is why many people hold grudges after being rejected.

I have watched the story of many people who are very physically appealing, intelligent, and maybe even wealthy, yet have very harsh attitudes. When asked to express their reasons for having a harsh demeanor, many have even traced it back to when they were rejected in school by their peers or family members. Many people go through life extremely guarded and somewhat paralyzed by past pain, so they won't have to open themselves up to the possibility of rejection again. Men and Women go from relationship to relationship, never settling down because they don't want to face the agony of being abandoned or vulnerable with anyone else because vulnerability leaves us wide open to the possibility of rejection. So, they live out the rest of their lives trying to avoid the hurt and pain of what they faced with ONE person.

I've been here also. It was like a cycle; Every chance I had when someone reached out to me, I would shut down and shrink back because of my past experiences. I wanted to get beyond it but just didn't know how. Through time with God, I began to inquire of Him what I should do when I realized that I was about to shrink back or alter my behavior because of rejection.

He told me to CHALLENGE IT!

BEAUTIFYING REJECTION: THE GREAT EXCHANGE

A strategy to get over shrinking back is taking a moment to challenge the fear of rejection by evaluating who we really are versus the poor treatment we have received in the past. If many of us would take the time to challenge the moment of rejection, we would see that even if we are not the best version of ourselves at the moment, despite anything, we deserve to be loved and respected. No matter what the rejection was about, it doesn't define us as a person. We are worthy of joy and acceptance. If not in the space of the person who rejected us, then we deserve it in another space.

But many of us don't challenge the fear of rejection. The better question is, why don't we?

Why don't we question the swirling thoughts of what others have said about us?

Why don't we question the tormenting thoughts of criticism from our past?

I asked myself these questions as I was going through my process. I realized that I didn't question these things and normally just assumed the responsibility, which is noble but not healing. I had to stare at myself and see that I didn't know how to challenge the fear of rejection or rejection itself because I didn't know the truth of God's word about me. When we don't have any truth of God to weigh the comments of others about ourselves against, we lay at the mercy of their rejection by default.

When we don't know the sweet voice of the Holy Spirit whispering...

"YOU ARE FEARFULLY AND WONDERFULLY MADE."
Psalms 139:14

Then when they say we are ugly, we will accept it.

When we don't know, **"We are made in the image and likeness of God"** Genesis 1:27

Then we will believe them when they say that we are nothing,

Warn Out & Disengaged

Since I didn't know God's word fully, I laid slaughtered in the residue of who others said I was. I heard the scriptures mentioned previously, and I could quote them...but I didn't KNOW them! I didn't have the type of relationship with the master that let the scriptures radiate in my mind and my heart, so out of that weakness I allowed the comments of others to hold me hostage.

I wept before the Lord but had not invited him into the room where my inner child laid. I had come to him in a holier than thou sort of way where I said a lot of words and preached to the walls, but I hadn't shown God my wombs in the secret place and allowed his loving salve to be smeared over me.

So, I sat there with head knowledge but nothing to truly comfort me. The only thing I could do to stop the darts of rejection from violently cutting me and jabbing me was to shut myself completely down and disengage. I could not allow anyone else in because I was too tender, and any other blows would have taken the little bit of life that I had left out of me. I was out, I was done for, and I was tired.

> *"...And he [enemy] shall speak great words against the most High, and shall wear out the saints of the most High..."*
> *Daniel 7:25a KJV*

No matter what, the enemy's goal is always to wear you out and to wear you down. The enemy hopes rejection will be enough to take you out or at least make you shut down to shut you up so that you won't be able to truly accomplish anything and live up to your highest potential.

Rejection comes back to remind you of past failures and traumas so that you will self-sabotage the progress that you have made and grow numb. The fear of rejection makes you hide when God calls you to shine, it makes you be quiet when you have the answers to speak, and it makes you run away when you have the potential to win the race. Fear of rejection is lethal, and its best friend is discouragement because when rejection jabs, discouragement tries to come at you disguised as a safety mechanism.

Discouragement says things like, "If they [those people that you think are better than you, more beautiful than you, richer than you] couldn't do it, then what makes you think you can? Just sit this one out, don't do it; you've been through enough."

Listening to these two, I sub-consciously built-up protective walls wrapped in barbed wire, gates armed by passivity, and a tongue loaded with ammo just in case I had trespassers. The bad part about this type of operation on the heart is that it could continue undetected under the protection guidelines and, more specifically, so-called "protecting my anointing."

I went through life accomplishing but never enjoying the accomplishment. Giving to others, thinking I was a friend but never truly receiving the love from the friend. I was the epitome of "Going through the motions."

I came to a space in life where I realized I wanted
> more... I wanted to feel joy.
> I wanted to laugh,
>> I wanted to speak without second-guessing.
>>> myself, I wanted to dance like nobody was
>>>> watching,
> I wanted to be FREE!

For so long, I numbed my emotions by focusing on my past, but God was about to sober me up in a way that only He could. God came through, removed the scales from my eyes, and pointed me to the mirror (if you engage with Him, He will engage with you). What He called me to do would require me to choose to face my thoughts and friend, I believe that is what He is calling you to do too.

I will share more with you in the Chapters ahead, but for now, I would like you to say this prayer below:

Prayer: *Father, thank you for this moment and journey thus far. Thank you that you are calling me to attention and showing me what idols I have engaged with and also what I have ignored. God, help me to see the idols that I have put over you and help me to obtain the strategies needed to overcome the plots of the enemy. In Jesus' name. Amen*

8

The Wake-Up Call: Accepting The Divine Plan Over Popularity

I had become self-righteous by depending on myself to protect myself; I turned off my emotions and made myself unavailable. Yea, I lied and said that the reason why I didn't spend time with others was that I was spending time with God and didn't have time for all of that. Interestingly enough, I did spend a lot of time in God's word, but I hadn't spent time in his heart and in a relationship with him. Even worse, the reason why I was so super spiritual and disconnected from others around me was not necessarily because of a spiritual reason but because I was scared to open up to others again, and I needed something to numb the pain of rejection. I spent time fantasizing about what I desired out of relationships and the outcomes I hoped to have. These fantasies consumed me just as much as the trauma of my rejection did. I called it "hoping in

God", yet theses desires were built from the anxieties of my past. I had over spiritualized it all because the truth is that it's easier to over-spiritualize our fears than it is to face them. I lived in a chronic state of listening to preaching sermons, labeling them "feeding my spirit," but honestly, I was really avoiding living life in the present moment. Sermon after sermon, I began to feel even more hopeless because I was eating the word at so many different tables that I created a concoction of goals and to-do lists, except for the goals that truly mattered.

Perhaps you can relate to my story of avoiding life and connectivity under the cover of religion or even avoiding a relationship with God because you're wondering why God would allow the type of pain you have suffered. Why would a loving God allow us to be the black sheep or the ones never counted into the party? Why would a loving God allow rejection to (seemingly) plague our existences?

Much like myself, maybe the aches and pains of rejection caused you to turn away from life's adventures and the Holy Spirit's invitation to change because you felt abandoned by God and inadequate by default.

Maybe the only hope that you have ever had in life was in your imagination.

Well-beloved, this is not the will of God, and quite frankly, God has much more for us than just imaginary scenarios of acceptance. So many of us imagine that boyfriend/girlfriend or ex-husband/ex-wife coming back completely changed, having realized that we are the only "one" for them.

...Or maybe that bully apologizing and affirming us.
... Or maybe our father or mother coming to love us in adulthood as they should have as a child.
...Or maybe some of us just want an apology for the violations we suffered at the hand of our violators.

These imaginary desires for a positive outcome can keep us bound to the pain of our past, just waiting for the affirmation to come. This is not the way that God wants us to walk through life, simply waiting for the change of hearts in other people. This mindset occupied me for many years and paralyzed me from experiencing life. That is, until one day, God challenged me to live in the moment.

At a holiday party of relatives, with newborn babies being passed around, plates being fixed completed with macaroni n' cheese and potato salad, there I was, sitting in the corner on top of a red cooler because there were no more chairs, near my immediate family, as I mindlessly strolled through my social media accounts. In the midst of a sea of voices laughing and talking, a football game, and soul music being played on the backyard patio, I heard a still, small voice say: "What if that never happens? What if you never get what you've been fantasizing about? What if they never recognize you as worthy or clap for your accomplishments? What if you are never perceived by them to be "good enough" for them to invite you to be a part of their click?"

At that moment, everything I hoped for and dreamed about crumbled to the ground of my heart. I felt these questions shake the very core of my belief systems.

With my thumb frozen in place on my iPhone and my eyes staring at the floor, the Holy Spirit rendered me speechless. I never considered that what my heart and mind hoped for wouldn't come to pass.

BEAUTIFYING REJECTION: THE GREAT EXCHANGE

Now I want you to pause and breathe because I pose to you the very same question.

"What if that never happens?"

What if you are never beautiful to them? What if you are never outgoing enough? What if you are never trendy enough? What if you are never loud enough for them to hear you? What if they never invite you to the party? What if you never know the inside joke? What if you are the inside joke? What if you never get that pat on the back? What if you are never the person they consider to be a friend, acquaintance, business partner, or soul mate? What if he/she never says "I love you"? What if they never see your value?

Take your time to think about this because I have to admit that these questions shook my imaginary world. I had held on to the hope that one day I would be good enough to fit in and that I would be invited to run out into the fields of daisies, roses, and sweet bliss. All of a sudden, here comes God bursting my bubble. My imagination was my only escape, and now God is telling me to face the fact that my one comfort might not be realistic.

I didn't have an answer. I had come to the end of my rope. Because of my constant rejection throughout my childhood, I had unconsciously made the object of my success their acceptance. This rendered me desperately acting out of a need and desire to be confirmed by those who had rejected me, making their validation the fuel of my motivation. Even worst, this constant pursuit had become my life's pursuit and yet a coping mechanism to deal with the pain of how inadequate I felt. I knew nothing else but the endless cycle of my need for validation and the performative nature of my deeds. Even though they never worked in making me whole, they would at least provide a momentary reprieve from what felt like the terminal illness in my soul named "rejection".

So here I sat on that little red cooler, present in the room but light years away in my heart, with the questions of God ringing in my years. This was my wit's end, the game of seeking their approval was in question, and its validity scrutinized in ways that only my heart could answer. It was time to stop running after the imaginary hope that rested on them and wake up to the reality as it was.

BEAUTIFYING REJECTION: THE GREAT EXCHANGE

Maybe you can identify. Like me, you have probably tried to do everything in your power to cope with the pain of rejection, but now you have come to the place where hoping it would end differently is no longer viable. Perhaps you have also come to the place in your walk of life where temporary fixes and dosages of validation just won't do.

Here is the good news; like me, this is precisely the place where God wants to speak to you!

So, there I was, at my wit's end, and God began to speak further, and here is what he said to me:

Bianca, have you ever considered that fitting in is not what I created you for? Fitting in would require the pieces that I adore about you to be clipped and smashed into something that my will for your life wouldn't recognize. You must remember that your destiny seeks the [authentic] you, not who you pretend to be and not who you hope will accept you. You have been working so hard to be their [people of this world] idea of perfection when I did not call you to find affirmation in the people. I called you to myself, and I am the one who will establish you. Even if the whole world falls at your feet and adorns you with every kind of earthy jewel, I am still the God of your heart who saturates you with peace and joy that never runs out. Even when the same world that praised your good works turns its back on you, I am still there with open arms and a peace that surpasses all understanding. I am literally more than the entire world against you. When you have me, you have everything you need, but without me, you have mere compliments and flattery, which feel good for a moment but fade into forgetfulness. Will you trust me to write out your destiny even when it means that Men will reject you? Do not make the desires of Men's love the object of your worship. Every time you imagine these things, you exalt the love of this world above me, which doesn't help you or Glorify Me. Wake up and realize that there is a beautiful life where I have placed you today, and no one can snatch that away from you unless you make the validation of man the object of your affection.

" Casting down imaginations, and every high thing that exalteth itself against the knowledge of God, and bringing into captivity every thought to the obedience of Christ..."
2 Corinthians 10:5 KJV

BEAUTIFYING REJECTION: THE GREAT EXCHANGE

I shared these sacred words with you because I believe that God is saying this to you today. Today at this very moment, realize that your desires to fit in are just that, desires, but God has already predestined and ordained you to be the authentic version of you, and the ordained version of you is what truly matters. Do not settle for pursuing the imaginary scenarios of acceptance when God has a beautiful life for you to experience now. I want you to reread the words, except write your name at the beginning and listen as God whispers in your ear as only He can. I'll see you in the next chapter.

_____have you ever considered that fitting in is not what I created you for? Fitting in would require the pieces that I adore about you to be clipped and smashed into something that my will for your life wouldn't recognize. You must remember that your destiny seeks the [authentic] you, not who you pretend to be and not who you hope will accept you. You have been working so hard to be their [people of this world] idea of perfection when I did not call you to find affirmation in the people. I called you to myself, and I am the one who will establish you. Even if the whole world falls at your feet and adorns you with every kind of earthy jewel, I am still the God of your heart who *saturates you with peace and joy that never runs out. Even when the same world that praised your good works turns its back on you, I am still there with open arms and a peace that surpasses all understanding. I am literally more than the entire world against you. When you have me, you have everything you need, but without me, you have mere compliments and flattery, which feel good for a moment but fade into forgetfulness. Will you trust me to write out your destiny even when it means that Men will reject you? Do not make the desires of Men's love the object of your worship. Every time you imagine these things, you exalt the love of this world above me, which doesn't help you or Glorify Me. Wake up and realize that there is a beautiful life where I have placed you today, and no one can snatch that away from you unless you make the validation of man the object of your affection.*

9

Own Your Ashes: Preparing for a Divine Exchange

God says He will give you beauty for ashes ...meaning He will give you something He owns for something you own but if you don't own the ashes then you have nothing to exchange.

One night (morning 2:00 am), I was up doing work and battling within myself about a recent occurrence that had taken place in my life. I was convinced that what transpired in my relationship with this person in particular was over betrayal, but Holy Spirit quickly challenged me to go deeper. I kept saying the word "but", with logical and valid responses to God; however, the Holy Spirit would not let up on me, and it began to weigh me down. Holy Spirit said, "Don't deflect from the part you played." I was brought to the scripture:

But if there is bitter jealousy or competition hiding in your heart, then don't deny it and try to compensate for it by boasting and being phony. For that has nothing to do with God's heavenly wisdom but can best be described as the wisdom of this world, both selfish[a] and devilish.[b] So wherever jealousy[c] and selfishness are uncovered, you will also find many troubles[d] and every kind of meanness.
James (Jacob) 3:14-16 TPT

As I read this scripture, wells of tears began to fill my eyes because I came to realize that some of the shambles of my ashes were a result of my own bitterness and jealousy. Even more so, I had taken bitterness a step further by denying the truth because I had justifiable reasons. I will say that God spoke to me and confirmed that the reasons I had for doing what I did in that relationship were valid, but he also held me accountable for the hidden jealousy in my heart. I had spoken to a few people about the relationship with this person in particular, and they agreed that my concerns were true and real. However, when you go before the Lord with a matter, He does not just look at facts; he also searches the heart. The truth was, it was easy for me to act in certain ways over small things because of the hidden jealousy and roots of bitterness. So, there I sat after over a year out of this situation happening, crying in my bed because Holy Spirit was calling me out of my denial. What truly hurt was that I had to admit that I had a problem; for months, I had carried the hurt and resentment because I didn't want to come to the realization of this truth.

In the middle of that moment, I heard God's still small voice say, "open your hands, physically, open your hands; you have been carrying the ashes of this dead relationship and your actions too long." The Lord continued to minister to me, saying, "Even though you played a part in burning it down to ashes, you are not those ashes."

If we are honest, many of the things that burn down in our life, whether that be marriage/family relationships, our health, friendships, or even financial means, are heavily a result of our actions or lack of action. Life can be so hard and difficult that sometimes the only option that we see is to set things on fire.

Maybe life gets so tough that we allow our tongue to spit out gulfs of fire onto people, or even out of our fears, we stand by and passively do nothing in complacency as the enemy takes over our camp and sets it ablaze. However, just because we experience these things doesn't mean we are what has burned down; we just need to own up to what is burned down within our life.

By this time, I had become aware that I was guilty of both burning things down and allowing them to burn. The super religious girl inside of me was triggered because the most painful reality for a person with a religious spirit is to realize that they are not perfect, have done wrong things, and still have things to work on. The only reason why the religious spirit had even inhabited me was through the doorway of an orphan spirit, which, put simply, is a spirit that makes one feel that they are fatherless/ motherless and that no one wants them. So, this set me on a path of trying to be perfect (calling it Holy) because the orphan girl in me was always trying to earn the love of God The Father through perfectionism, but God pointing out my wrong made me feel that I had failed. Those who struggle with an orphan spirit (like I had) typically try to overcompensate by doing everything just right in the hope of validation, acceptance, and approval; when the spirit of perfectionism mixes with a false doctrine of Christ's acceptance of his children, it turns into a lethal religious spirit. At that moment, God's confrontation of my wrongdoing wasn't just a correction; it was a call to repentance from who I had become and from the perfectionism that I had depended on to validate my legitimacy as a daughter of God.

The dusty place

Listen, the phrase "the truth hurts" had become the epitome of what I felt in every fiber of my being. I had been cornered with nowhere to turn to but to the throne of God's mercy. By this time, all I wanted was to go to the kitchen, eat a cookie, and eat a few chips to wash down my tears. I just didn't know how I was supposed to cope with the truth of my imperfection. But what I love about God's still small voice is that it won't quit on you even when you feel that you are in a moment that is unbearable.

God continued to speak to my heart as I sat with my legs crisscrossed, eyes shut, and tears streaming down my face without a tissue in sight. He said, "Just because the ashes came from your grounds doesn't mean that I can't grow something even more beautiful there, open your hands."

I found out the privilege of owning your mess is that once you do, God will allow you to exchange it for something beautiful. While my feelings searched for a place to put the pain of my ashes, God instructed me on the best place for them. For weeks I had been hearing the words "let it go," and I was really trying too. Every time something from an old situation came up, I would tell myself just get over it and let it go. This worked only for a while until God showed me that ashes are not supposed to be suppressed; they are to be cleaned up.

God showed me how I had been sweeping my true feelings under the rug and calling it letting go, but just because you can't see it doesn't mean it's gone; it's just hidden. My biggest pain point and concern was where to put the ashes of what failed in my life, and the Lord said, "The reason why those ashes exist and are more plentiful is because you became a holding place for other people's ashes too. You held on to what others said about you, who they said you needed to be, what they said you would never be, and how they rejected you. The sparks of other people's bitterness kindled ideas, perspectives, and concepts in you and about you, which served as the breeding ground for your destruction in your heart."

When God told me to pay attention to the part of the ashes in my hands, it didn't mean that the spark that caused the fire didn't also receive its bearings in the world. God knows that situations can put us in crazy spaces, but he also knows that if we don't take inventory of our actions and more importantly, our hearts, then we will never be able to stop the spread of spiritual wildfires.

As I continued to hold my hands open, "the Lord said, "Even as I collect your tears, I am collecting every piece of ash in your heart. Whether the ash came from your fire or their fires, I want them all, failed relationships, ventures, even your feelings of unworthiness. I am throwing your wrong deeds into the sea of forgetfulness, and your only responsibility is the commitment to give me the ashes."

Restoration

After God said all of this, I heard him say, "You're dirty; you've got rubbish and ashes all over you, but the trash on top of the ground cannot diminish the value of the property." Any wealth strategist will tell you that one of the best investments you will ever make is in real estate and owning property simply because the market can never create more land. God was saying to me that I was still good ground no matter what had happened and taken place in life, and SO ARE YOU! Furthermore, there is nothing a homeowner can do with the ashes of a home that has burned down except clean the ground and rebuild. In this moment with God, I realize that the reason why I was so burdened down was that I was holding onto what no longer served my sustainability.

I heard God say, "You are good ground, and many may see ashes on you now, but soon I will set my glory on you. Where many see weeds, I will carve into a work of art as though I am an arborist."

Not only did God want to clean up my heart and life, but he also wanted to use it to showcase his glory.

This moment was very painful, so I do not share this as simply another story to fill the pages of this book. I share this moment with you as a challenge for you to also find the hidden things in your heart that would cause you to burn down the things that God wants to bless you with in your future. Ask the Holy Spirit to walk you through your dusty place so that you can open your hands and give Him the ashes, the things that no longer sustain you, over to God. This is by no means an easy process; some of the ashes could almost cause you to choke on the aroma of them because of the memory of them but you must remember that those ashes in God's eyes are the currency of manifesting His beauty.

Prayer: Lord, I thank you for being a father that confronts our hearts out of your love for us. I thank you for both the beautiful moments of favor and the moments of rebuke. Lord, whatever you do, don't let us be turned over to our filth. Show us what pleases you, and when we fall short, we thank you for pointing it out and building our character. I ask you to cover our hearts and stabilize us in your love as we take ownership and increase in integrity. Show us how to walk through this moment and release every speck of ash to you. We surrender it all to you right now. In the name of Jesus. Amen.

10

Dismantling Disaster: Making Way for God's Newness

Recently on a trip back to my home city of Houston, Tx, on my way to my grandmother's home, I passed by a neighborhood, and just at the edge of the neighborhood, I saw cleared land with grass budding. This caught my eye specifically because the last time I was in my old neighborhood, I passed by this same space while there was a huge fire burning protruding from the house that was on this very land. The fire burned so greatly that the smoke could be seen for miles, and as I passed by the house across from the fire, the flames were so hot that I could feel the heat while pressing my fingers up against my car window.

What is even more interesting is that I had never seen this home before or even looked its way ever. Just like in life, we never really start staring at something until something special or terrible happens to it. My first glimpse of this beautiful home was while a disaster was happening. I'm pretty sure that the owner must have felt devastated but also vulnerable. Limb by limb, everything the owners worked for was crumbling and burning up before them and everyone else passing by. As the firefighters rushed in to contain the fire, I began thinking about the one time I almost burned my family's house down as a preteen. I was cooking on our gas stove while my family was gone to work one summer, and I didn't realize that I had left a potholder near the lit burner.

At the sink, I smelled smoke and turned around to see the potholder on fire. Fully panicked and afraid, I rushed to the stove, grabbed the lit potholder, and somehow put out the fire (it was definitely a work of God because to this day I have no idea how I did that).

What strikes me about that horrible experience is that at that moment, I didn't just think about us losing our home; I mostly thought about it being my fault, my mistake, and the pain I would cause. I was so embarrassed about that experience that I have never told anyone about that until now. I was more embarrassed to be exposed as making a mistake and hurting my family than anything else. Undoubtedly when I looked back at that house fire that I was passing by I can almost hear someone saying, "I'm sorry, I made a mistake."

Many of the fires in our life come from mistakes that we or other people near us make, and sometimes it can be hard to get beyond the mistakes (like me with my potholder on fire). However, healing on the land can only come when we deal with the structure that was burned in the fire. The land is still usable, but the structure must be torn down and dismantled appropriately in order to revitalize the land.

Just like this land, you are good ground, but there are places within your life where you have experienced disaster in the form of rejection. Maybe it even came from you rejecting yourself or God's plans for your life. It's time to dismantle the structures of what used to work in your life but what no longer serves your future. Maybe that structure is in the form of how you dealt with past relationships or even how you dealt with yourself, and it worked until sparks started flying. Now you look at that structure as the greatness of what was, and you blame yourself for its demise, but if you continue to stare at it, you will miss the newness that God wants to grow in your life.

"Behold, I will do a new thing; now it shall spring forth; shall ye not know it? I will even make a way in the wilderness, and rivers in the desert."
Isaiah 43:19 ASV

We don't always realize that allowing something to remain in our lives past its use or expiration date only creates dead monuments and blocks the space for us to grow and flourish.

I have been somewhat vague in defining what the structure is because I respect that for some of you, your structure may be the pattern in which you think or talk about yourself. For others, it may be the constant rehearsal of the loss of relationships, while for some a faulty operating belief system. Whatever that structure in your life is, I want you to identify it and tear it down, even if you have to do it brick by brick or nail by nail. I recommend talking to a Christian counselor or trusted confidant who can aid you in sorting through the painful trauma and rubble of this structure.

Just like the land I passed, with brown patches in some areas and hopeful green patches budding in others, I pray that you see the restoration of your heart as you clear the grounds of your heart. There is new life waiting on the other side of tearing down old structures, and I believe that it is yours today.

Pray with me:
Heavenly Father, thank you for breaking through the pain of what I lost to make me realize that the loss of that structure is not the loss of everything, even though it hurts. Forgive me for only nursing the pain of that place and help me to move beyond my pain to see a fresh tomorrow. Help me forgive myself and those who may have made the mistakes that led me here. I ask you to help me identify those who are anointed to see the bigger picture than I can see right now and help me take the journey to healing. In Jesus' name. Amen

11

Interlude: Let's Take A Break

Let's do an Exercise together (Yes, NOW).

At this moment, as you breathe in slowly through your nose and breathe out through your mouth, I want you to MENTALLY imagine going into your mind. Now close the door of your rational thinking and open the door to allow God to come in and examine your heart and your ways. As you breathe out, release the need to be perfect and breathing in the belief that God is doing a great work in you even as you read this. Inhale the goodness of God and how much He loves you.

Now, I know you may be thinking, "Why are we doing this?"

We are doing this because we are about to go to another part of the healing process, and I want you to be able to do this exercise every time we get to a place in the book that becomes a little rocky for you. I want you to know that typically the hardest lessons to hear or to absorb are the very ones that set us free. This is evident in the occurrences that some of the best medicines usually taste the worst, and spiritual medicines sometimes taste just as bitter. We also know that alcohol stings, but it only stings when it comes in contact with the wounded area of the body. Even with all of that, it's one of the most used cleansing agents because in spite of the sting, it's extremely effective at preventing infections.

Now, some may say, "This is not a physical wound; it's a broken heart problem," and partially, they are right because while a broken heart is a soul problem, it typically manifests in the natural as well. However, I want to reach beyond your logic and grab the hand of the part of you that's desperate for the healing touch that will make you whole. You are not reading this by accident; you're reading it because you want solutions, and you want to be healed. So even if it stings a little (like it stung me), it's okay; "You will live"!

No, really, YOU WILL LIVE! The promise of your better life is this way… Let's Go!

Let me pray for you.

Prayer: Lord God, I pray for your liberating power to rest over the person reading these words right now. I pray for freedom rooted in you that would cause them to walk in the mind of Christ. I pray for a spirit of courage to rise in them and continue onto the next phase of their healing process. Let them not be weary in well doing but sit in a place of peace as the Holy Spirit in them pace their hearts towards becoming a whole person. Secure them in only a way that you can and remind them of your presence at every turn. We thank you for your grace and mercy that has led us here, and that will continue to lead us forward. All this I ask in Jesus' name. Amen

12

Divine Sufficiency: Living In God's Abundance

> The thief cometh not but to steal and to kill and to destroy. I am come that they might have life, and that they might have it more abundantly.
> John 10:10 KJV

In order for us to get the true meaning of abundant life (which is something I know that you want if you are reading this book), we have to go a little deeper.

The phrase "abundant life" in the original scripture was actually the Greek term "Perissos." Many times, in the Bible, one word is used interchangeably in different areas, and so it is with this term that I encourage you to study more in-depth. The Greek word Perissos pertaining to the abundance of life, has several meanings, such as:

exceedingly some number or measure or rank or need over and above, more than is necessary, superadded exceedingly abundantly, supremely something further, more, much more than all, more plainly superior, extraordinary, surpassing, uncommon pre-eminence, superiority, advantage, more eminent, more remarkable, more excellent.

Let's make it plain: abundance is every definition above. Abundant life is an over and above life; it's an extraordinary life, an uncommon life, an advantaged life, a remarkable life, a more excellent life! Abundant life is over and beyond a normalized existence. It is all about experiencing life not without trials that reside in the human experience, but beyond the limits and confinements of our human barriers.

Abundant life Unnoticed

Many times, we neglect to identify abundant life at work in our life because it's not always recognized according to what is typically taught about abundant life. Sadly, abundant life has been deemed several things, and some teachings have even caused many misconceptions in Christendom that ultimately lead to disappointment, such as:

BEAUTIFYING REJECTION: THE GREAT EXCHANGE

- If I have God, then I have abundant life, therefore my life will be perfect
- If I have an abundant life then I will do everything perfect
- Abundant life means that I will never go through trials
- Abundant life means that I don't have frustrating moments

Now that we have exposed those myths, you should know that abundant life isn't about having some dystopia of no obstacles, aches, trials, or pain (That dystopia actually exists, and it's called Heaven, but that's for another book...just thought I would say something). Check out this scripture:

"But now I go my way to Him that sent Me; and none of you asks me, Where are you going? But because I have said these things unto you, sorrow has filled your heart."
John 16:5-6

"I have told you these things, so that in me you may have peace. In this world, you will have trouble. But take heart! I have overcome the world."
John 16: NIV

In this passage of scripture, Jesus is speaking to his disciples and giving them insight into the plan of God that is about to take place. He tells His disciples that He is about to go back to the Father in Heaven; now, this is a very traumatic revelation for the disciples at the time (Yes, sometimes the revelation of God can be traumatic) because this means that Jesus will no longer be with the disciples in the flesh.

Think about this: can you imagine giving up everything you have, including your family, your friends, and your occupation, to follow a man and work in their ministry? You completely abandon everything you ever knew in exchange for following a cause and a mission built around one man, and then the person you have built your life around says they are about to leave the earth?

I know some would say, "Well, it was Jesus, so it shouldn't be that bad," and I somewhat agree with them because the Bible encourages us to follow God and be relentless. However, we must not neglect the context of the unforeseen circumstances which surrounded the disciples in this passage of scripture. The disciples were not privileged to have a Bible like us, nor did they have the Holy Spirit to reveal things to them, as the Holy Spirit (who knows all things) was not set to come until after Jesus' departure back to the Father. So, with that in mind, all the disciples had to hold onto was knowing and walking with Jesus!

All Peter knew was that God came to him while he was on the boat and said, "Come with me, and I'll make you fishers of man."

All Philip knew was that Jesus found him and said, "Follow me."

All Nathanael knew was that Phillip told him they had found the Messiah, and even though he was skeptical, he went to meet Jesus. In his skepticism, Jesus appeals to him and says He saw him under the fig tree, and that is how He perceives Him to be the Messiah.

All they knew was a physical Jesus, and at this moment, we see a depiction of the One they left it all for, saying that He is leaving to go back to the Father in Heaven.

Here they are with the promises of abundant life, and yet it feels that it could all be lost. Have you ever been through moments where you felt like you were losing a person or something you heavily depended on?

I have, and it is perhaps one of the most painful losses there is. I went through this in several instances; one of the more painful was the sudden loss of my mom at the age of 22. Losses are hard in general, but even more so when the loss is sudden. These kinds of losses feel like a violent ripping away of a part of your heart for which you have no replacement—leaving a person alone to nurse a wound that they could have never been prepared for.

With this perspective, we can identify with the disciples. I believe this is why Simon Peter reacted in such a vitriolic way in John 18 when the Roman soldiers came to get Jesus so that they could crucify Him. Peter was so upset that he took a sword and cut off the ear of the Roman soldier because he didn't want Jesus to be apprehended. Then Jesus heals the soldier and tells Simon Peter, "Get behind me, Satan."

For a long time as a young lady, I couldn't understand why Jesus said, "Get behind me, Satan," to dear Peter. Didn't Jesus see that Peter just loved him and wanted him to remain safe? It seemed like Peter was only trying to be a good friend and defend him, right? Well, not exactly.

I believe that Peter's actions erupted from the places of his own fear. I believe that because He knew the day was near when he would have to really walk out the Gospel without Jesus in the flesh, He was afraid. At this moment, Peter seemed strong-willed and fearless by cutting the soldier's ear off, but really, He was operating in a faithless and fearful state. Peter's fear response was to fight; it wasn't as though he was surprised because Jesus warned the disciples of what was to come before it took place.

Sidebar: Isn't it amazing that even one of Jesus' close disciples and friends was afraid and acted out of it? Let this alleviate you of feeling like you are the only person in the world who falls short. "... for all have sinned and fall short of the glory of God.." Romans 3:23 *ESV*

Peter was scared to lose Jesus and, even more, afraid of bearing the cross that would come along with the next phase of his journey as a leader in the church.

If all of this is not enough, Jesus also tells them in John 16 how they will be persecuted while preaching the gospel of Jesus. He ends this passage by telling them that he has given them insight because they will experience tribulation.

Tribulation is not the absence of abundance.

When you go through deep waters, I will be with you.
When you go through rivers of difficulty, you will not drown.
When you walk through the fire of oppression, you will not be burned up;
the flames will not consume you.
Isaiah 43:2 NLT
Then Jesus told his disciples, "If anyone would come after me, let him deny himself and take up his cross and follow me.
Matthew 16:24-26 ESV

To be clothed in humanity is to experience the consequences of the falling of Mankind, but experiencing the pain of the human experience does not mean we have been disqualified from experiencing the abundant joy of walking through the pain with Jesus. Oh, how privileged we are to have a Father in heaven who will not leave us to our own demise, but He also makes a promise to be present through it all and walk with us as we deny ourselves and follow Him. The gift of abundant life is the promise that when you go through the rejection of man, you are not walking alone. You are walking with a God who has been through it all and has overcome it all.

The gift of abundant life is not the absence of trials but, indeed, recognizing that abundance itself resides in the Lord! This is how He is able to give us the overcoming gift of abundant life. The gift calls you up higher than the rejection. The gift of abundant life gives you a new perspective through a renewed mind and a clean heart. This gift brings hope and enlightenment!

This walk with Christ is not a cakewalk in the park at all: However, the thought of walking this life alone without Jesus is even more treacherous. I would prefer to walk with God, knowing that I will ultimately go through trials but still be privileged to walk with the Lord God, who says, "Cheer up for I have overcome the world" John 16:33.

Live in the abundance

As I bring this chapter to a close, never neglect to know that no matter what or who you perceive to lose, God is always more than the world against you. If He is for you, then there is no one, nothing, and no lie that can come against you. The very presence of the Lord in your life is all of the abundances that you will ever need. Place your hope and expectation in the Lord, for there is no lack in the Father.

"And let patience have its perfect work, that ye may be perfect and entire, lacking in nothing."
James 1:4 American Standard Version (ASV)

When your heart begins to become weary in welldoing as you wait on the manifestation of abundance, I want you to take something with you. I heard Pastor Dennis Jones say, "Confusion [or anxiousness] comes from what you are waiting on [to happen], but comfort comes from who you're waiting on."

Since we know that God is with us, He has promised us abundant life, and that He is a faithful God, then we must confess what Psalm 27:13- 14 says:

> I remain confident of this:
> I will see the goodness of the Lord in the land of the living.
> Wait for the Lord;
> be strong and take heart and wait for the Lord.
> Psalm 27:13-14 *NIV*

Believe God has abundant life and that you live in it because you live in him and that this is your inheritance as a child of God! I end this chapter with this prayer found in Ephesians 1:18 *NIV*.

"I pray that the eyes of your heart may be enlightened in order that you may know the hope to which he has called you, the riches of his glorious inheritance in his holy people…"

13

Heart's Eclipse: The Shadow Of Self-Condemnation

One of the secret gems that I have learned along the way as it relates to beauty and the heart is that the enemy likes to infect our hearts so that we do not shine with the radiance of God. Because we view life and circumstances through the lens of our heart, when we live with broken hearts shattered by rejection, we become fragmented in our thinking and perception.

Recently, I spoke at a virtual conference on a dynamic topic that had me focus on doing what God desires for us to do. During my study on this topic, I discovered so much about guilt, and how paralyzing it can be to the plans of God over our lives. God gave me revelation pertaining to guilt and showed me how the heart receives guilt.

Firstly, guilt is a burden sent by the enemy, and it can only get in through our permission and our actions. Guilt's sole job is to build a case against us in our own hearts so that we begin to feel unworthy to go on and walk into the promises of God. Guilt is actually the gateway to shame, and then shame becomes the gateway to condemnation. Instead of the conviction to change and become more like Christ, the enemy tries to infect our hearts with the prison of condemnation, which serves as a pit of self-hatred. The enemy does this because he knows that by infecting our hearts with guilt, we cannot fully walk in God's promises because, in this space, we cannot take the correct actions according to God's grace and faithfulness.

The Heart

The heart is the place we take action and live our lives from.

For each tree is known by its own fruit. Indeed, figs are not gathered from thornbushes, nor grapes from brambles. The good man brings good things out of the good treasure of his heart, and the evil man brings evil things out of the evil treasure of his heart.
For out of the overflow of the heart, the mouth speaks.
Luke 6:44-45 BSB

For this reason, our heart is the single most important determinant of us understanding our actions. For the scripture says:

*"As a **man** thinketh in **his heart**, so is he"*
Proverbs 23:7 KJV

You brood of vipers! How can you speak good things, when you are evil? For out of the abundance of the heart the mouth speaks.
Matthew 24

We act and make decisions from the heart; our hearts are the epicenter of our goals and deeds, and if that part of us is tainted, we become the tragedy of our own broken hearts. Our heart even affects our sensibility in our relationships. Instead of hearing our family and friends through the filter of love, we hear them through the blockage of rejection. This has happened to me many times where friends have said things to me even in a joking way, and instead of it bringing me joy, I immediately became defensive. Perhaps you have been in this place as I have, where all things feel insulting and isolating when they should feel lite and as something we can release as fast as they come at us. The problem is when our hearts are infected, we are unable to walk through life freely.

When we live in a place of brokenness, we go from living to surviving, which then causes us to become extra sensitive. If anything, similar to a threat comes close to us, we tend to annihilate it before it can annihilate us. This is the mindset of a soldier in a war zone, "Kill them before they can kill you." At the very least, we shut the door on relationships and opportunities "just in case" they may try something.

But this is no way to live!

God didn't call us so that we could be in a constant battle and war zone, peeping around every corner to see who would potentially hurt us next. Staying locked and loaded with the bullets of snapping on people and going off....Noooo... that's not living! The word of God says:

"The thief comes only to steal and kill and destroy; I came that they may have life, and have it abundantly.
John 10:10 NAS

14

Nourishing The Heart: Cultivating Your Inner Sanctuary

"For as he thinks in his heart, so is he [in behavior—
one who manipulates].
He says to you, "Eat and drink,"
Yet his heart is not with you [but it is begrudging the
cost]."
Proverbs 23:7 Amplified Bible

My heart had been poisoned by the opinions and perspectives of the enemy, which were sent to keep me trapped and insecure. However, after blaming the devil and his demons, there comes a time when we must take responsibility for the space, we give them in our lives and in our hearts.

The first place that I began evaluating my heart was with my thoughts because even though I had the knowledge of God, poisonous thoughts have a sneaky little way of trying to coexist with the Knowledge of

God. I lived many years like this, so I know that just because we get knowledge doesn't mean we operate in its wisdom by applying it.

When I examined my thoughts, I realized that they had not been lining up with the knowledge of Christ and what I was told God had for me. I had opened my heart to the judgment of this world and sent my heart out as the Ransom that paid for my lack of guarding myself. No wonder I was so off track! My mind was scattered, and my heart was shattered, and yet, I was tired of it! I was fed up with being mad at the devil when my Bible said that there was healing available and that I was no longer a slave to sin. I needed to know what to do... but my only question was, "how"? How could I cover my heart and regulate my mind again? How could I take back my sanity from the enemy that I had allowed to rule over me for so long?

I knew there were no quick fixes, but I also knew that if I didn't find relief for my aching heart and medicine to combat the sickness that came from the orphan spirit, I would not make it another week. Between the depression, insecurities, and my shortcomings, I needed God to show me how to cope and lovingly accept the place where I was.

The Bubble Strategy

What thoughts could I think that would cause me to agree and align with my destiny and what God says about me?

How could I stabilize my mind and heart even though I still needed to go through the healing process?

These were the scriptures that came to mind:

"Take the helmet of salvation and the sword of the Spirit, which is the word of God."
Ephesians 6:17 NIV

"Set your minds on things above, not on earthly things..."
Colossians 3:2 NIV

"Let this mind be in you, which was also in Christ Jesus"
Philippians 2:5 KJV

This is where God began speaking to me about the strategy of getting under the hedge.

Over my lifetime, I tended to be very extreme, either very open or very closed off, with no balance. So, when God started speaking about protection, I truly thought that I had tried everything I could to the point that I felt hopeless and like a sitting duck. On my way to work one morning during rush hour traffic, I heard the Lord say "demarcation." I must admit that when I heard it, I had never seen or known the word before, so I looked it up, and here is what it means:

de·mar·ca·tion
/1dēmär1kāSH(ə)n/ : a dividing line.

In my oh-so-churchy, pre-pandemic way, I said God is about to set things straight. When you're religious, it's easier to think of God as a superhero getting everything and everyone else straight instead of your Lord calling you to get disciplined and set yourself straight. It took me three years to find out that God wanted me to draw the line and set boundaries for my heart. His superhero moment was done on the cross for us when He died for our sins, and now he is sitting at the right hand of the Father. He died so that we would be able to stand boldly before the throne of grace and take up the original authority that God gave to men when he created us.

Pappa-God was not coming down off the throne of heaven to draw lines and boundaries for me that he had sent his son to die and give me authority over. It was up to me to allow his truth to ring louder than my immediate thoughts and fears. I would have to accept the belief system of God and be willing to wear what the Bible says is "the helmet of salvation," which is the word of God, resulting in a hedge of protection from the lies of Satan.

The word of God says let this mind be in you that is also in Christ Jesus. (Philippians 2:5). This means we must allow ourselves to be submerged in the mind of Christ, which is the word of God!
In His thoughts
  In His ideas…
    In His concepts…
      In His truth…
The healing process can be overwhelming, and if we depend on our feelings while going through the depth of our broken hearts, then we will surely drown as it cuts off our oxygen to the life-given properties of joy. However, while we go through the process, if we wear

the helmet of salvation, which is God's word, we create a bubble and barrier for our mind, not allowing it to be tainted by the brokenness of our hearts. In order to go through the process, we need the oxygen of God's word to remain stable enough to heal through it.

When scuba divers dive into deep sea spaces for long periods of time they do so with a helmet to not just make sure they are covered from the elements of which they must operate but also to be able to breathe and receive oxygen efficiently. I realized that if I was going to survive this difficult place that I had gotten into, I would have to secure my head with God's hedge of protection. I would have to be so covered in God's word as if it was the only way I could breathe and get oxygen. Even as a scuba divers helmet, I would be able to see and examine myself and yet get my breath on the inside of God's word and protection. This is necessary because we need the word of God to bring us new thoughts, like giving our body new oxygen.

Prayer: Lord, I thank you for equipping my kingdom sibling with what is needed to heal but also what is needed to be stable through the healing process. Lord, I pray that they would continuously abide in the word and that nothing shall be able to shake them because they are secure in the word of God. In Jesus' name, Amen.

15

Breathing Life: The Thoughts That Sustain Our Hearts

As a child, I suffered terribly from Asthma, so much so that I almost died during several Asthma attacks. I spent most of my evenings with inhalers and equipment that cleaned the air and helped me to continue to breathe. One of the things that is recommended is to clean the oxygen equipment from contamination and pollutants routinely. If not, it could cause additional issues and could cause a person to get respiratory infections which would cause the illness to get worse. In many cases, infections aren't a result of the oxygen in the tank, but most of the time, a person can be susceptible to contamination if a cannula, which is the clear tube that creates the airflow from the tank to the body, is contaminated.

If the Cannula is contaminated, then the oxygen will mix with the contaminants, thus creating infections. In my case, my asthma attacks were not a result of the oxygen that was meant to supply me with life, but they could have been attributed to a mixture that contaminated the machine and almost caused premature death.

Like the Cannula of an oxygen device, our thoughts form and create the pathway to the life we have. The breath can be present such as scriptures, knowledge, and information. As a matter of fact, scripture is called " the breath of God," as in 2 Timothy 3:16.

All Scripture is God-breathed(A) and is useful for teaching,(B) rebuking, correcting and training in righteousness,(C) so that the servant of God[a](D) may be thoroughly equipped for every good work.(E)
2 Timothy 3:16-17

You may be like me in a situation where you know the word of God and soak up information all the time. However, you can't figure out why you may feel that life is not getting better, and in fact, you may feel even more discouraged than you ever have before, even though you know God's breath of life, the word. I found out that sometimes we continue to live a defeated life with a defeated mindset because of what's transporting the word of God and the possible contamination.

I realize that my biggest issue of why the word wasn't working in my life was because I was breathing in the oxygen of God's word simultaneously with worldly debris that was harmful to me. I would spend time with God and then return to listening to worldly inspiration and rhetoric based upon a consciousness that stood in direct conflict with THE TRUTH of God. There is always danger when we mix the uncompromising breath of God with other things that are not of God. God's word must be the only focus in our life because it is the only agent that can produce life and life more abundantly. The polluted perspectives of this world are harmful because they come to block the flow of Christ's purity in our life. God intends for us to live whole and to love Him and be confident, not self-loathing, not depressed, and certainly not confused about who we are.

But how does this happen... how do pollutants get here? ... Because certainly none of us would allow ourselves to intentionally get emotionally sick or downcast. Everyone wants to live well and breathe well, that's the reason why we go to the word of God, right?

So how do we clean the pathway so that we can breathe in peace again?

Let this mind be in you, which was also in Christ Jesus
Philippians 2:5

We do it by changing and elevating our thoughts to think God's thoughts found in His word. We rid ourselves of what no longer serves our soul and the plan of God by submerging in the sea of God's word with God. The key to allowing this to work in our lives is by being uncompromising in our submergence in the word of Christ and not being deterred by what we see around us.

Submerge yourself in God - Development

The ideas we choose to submerge in either give life to the mind of Christ in us or take away its authority to operate in us. It is that split second of path selection that steers us into destiny and the belief that we can be who God calls us to be versus choosing the pattern and path of rejection.

Again, nobody wants to truly go against God because we were created to inherently want what God has for us. What I am sharing with you is not about you saying, "Okay, I'm going to be disciplined and just do it." No, it's about **DEVELOPING** a thought pattern that will foster the fruit that only the applied breath of God can produce. This is where the rubber meets the road, and we govern ourselves upon a solid foundation that is the word of God.

Honestly, it has been my experience that the only time most of us get off track is because of discouragement and the desires we want to happen. Many times, I only began to mix the word of God with other practices outside of his word because I had lifted my desires above my desire for God, thus creating a mindset where I would do anything to get what I wanted, including adopting thoughts and mentalities that never came from God. I followed people that were manifesting instead of praying, people who used crystals instead of pleading the blood of Jesus, and people who asked the universe instead of the creator of the universe.

"Do not love the world nor the things in the world. If anyone loves the world, the love of the Father is not in him. For all that is in the world, the lust of the flesh and the lust of the eyes and the boastful pride of life, is not from the Father, but is from the world. The world is passing away and also its lusts; but the one who does the will of God continues to live forever."
1 John 2: 15-17, NASB

The lust I had for my desires to be fulfilled led me astray and almost suffocated me out of an abundant life that God had already promised His children would have.

The Bible says, "Let this mind be in you" the word "let" is a word that causes us to make a decision to allow things to be so in our life. This says to me that the mind of Christ is available, but it must be received and allowed to reside. Even more than that, it also says that there are conditions that must be made for the mind of Christ to reside in us. I believe that the condition required to let it be is total surrender to the mind of Christ.

I have learned that God's breath does not need another agent to help it work, but it is our responsibility as children of God to stand firm in belief and expectation without wavering. Even when we see on the outside of us that nothing else has shifted or changed for us, we must refuse to cross-contaminate the mind of Christ with the ideas of this world. When we fully submerge and surrender ourselves to Christ, we correct the passageways of our receiving and clear the way so that the breath of God can really empower us as only He can do.

16

Shedding the Victim's Cloak: Embracing Divine Empowerment

For much of my life, I lived with a victim mindset. This victim mentality enabled me to rebuttal God's call to be humble in prayer as something that I was exempt from on the basis of me always feeling rejected. I felt that being bullied in school, romantically rejected, and seemingly a black sheep qualified me as being humbled enough. I mean, for goodness sake, I had been constantly bullied and used as a doormat for most of my life. Really, how low can one person really go? So I thought that I had the humbleness aspect together! Right? Well, not exactly!

I had made a significant mistake that I see many who constantly suffer from rejection make. I engaged in the spirit of victimization, where I allowed my wounds of rejection to become my God. I had come to a point where I equated the pain of rejection to righteous suffering and believed that God would bless me because of it; after all, what kind of God wouldn't help a victim?

I went through life constantly nursing my wounds as if the word of God didn't say (and it does) in John 16:33, "I have told you these things, so that in me you may have peace. In this world, you will have trouble. But take heart! I have overcome the world."

For a while, coming to God as a constant victim worked for me in God's presence, where God's spirit comforted me, and then I went away and felt okay. However, I kept having to come back again and again and be comforted when yet another rejection from a person came my way. I went through the cycle of rejection continually, where I was told in the presence of God that I was beautiful and that I was enough, and then something else would happen, and I would feel hopeless, depressed, and worthless all over again. Eventually, I came to a point where I wondered if I would ever be free and go on to my promised destiny.

It seemed like I just couldn't get up out of the state of feeling pitiful, and I needed to know why!

Then the Lord spoke to me and said, "The reason why you haven't been able to come out of this is that you're operating in a spirit of victimization. You have a right to feel that you have been a victim in many instances, but if you make it your identity, then you only have access to the privileges of victims but not whole people."

Whewww... didn't see that coming.

I found out that if we remain a victim, only paying attention to who and how others have treated us, we will always be waiting on the reward of a victim. However, if we stay there, we will never be able to receive the promise of God because the promises of God require wholeness. We must cast aside the spirit of victimization because entertaining it can breed a sense of entitlement. There have been times when I have been guilty of feeling justified in being entitled due to the wounds of rejection. I would allow rejection to caress my ego into making a decision beneath the promises of God because I felt that my life had been hard enough anyway, so why go the extra mile? As if the wounds of my past justified poor behavior.

This precisely is how many of us who have gone through childhood and early life traumas end up recommitting some of the same injustices and mistakes in our later life. We don't heal from the issues of our past, so we carry it into our future. We then reach for those wounds as our justification and support to carry all the shame for our poor choices. When faced with spiritually immoral dilemmas and consequences, we tend to say things like, "This is what I've seen all my life, and this is how I was treated as a child," and we continue shattering innocent victims' lives. We never stop to see that what we really desire is justice for the injustices committed to us, and because we go through life dishing out to others what is killing us in our hearts, we become the unaccountable bullies that terrorize us.

This lifestyle is both debilitating and unstable. I have been here in this place of mixed emotions where it seems like I could never stay in a mentally neutral mindset, constantly dissecting the words of other people around me. Of course, not able to trust anyone with walls built up 10 feet high. Yet in my heart, I secretly prayed to God for people who could see past my defensive nature.

The scary part of this is that during this time that I engaged in false humility, I was a believer in Christ serving in my community church. I made sure that I never missed a Sunday, and I worked in most of the church activity groups, yet I was still chained to my victimization. I used the things I had been through, such as bullying and even divorce, to feed my high-minded piousness, which is only a false sense of Godliness.

What happened is that I allowed my wounds to become my God, saying things like "I've been through too much hell," as if it was a badge of sufferance. I didn't recognize that the boasting of my rejection in my mind had become my only existence and my salvation.

However, this is not the way God has intended for us to live. In paraphrasing, 2 Corinthians 10:5 says for us to cast down every high thing that would exalt itself against the knowledge of God. We must humble ourselves into realizing that even our pains are subject to the greatness of God. After going through years of rejection, I could only identify myself through the lens of oppression, which became my muse. I would hear the word of God that said I was victorious and still not grasp it and not proclaim it because I was the slave of my suffering; never once did I think that it was a sin.

It was a sin to make rejection my badge of piety because to invest our identity into anything other than what God has stated about us is not only a sin but a hindrance keeping us from walking in the promises of God. I could listen to the word of God all day, but if I did not humble my mind and my will, I would continue to be an unstable woman going through life in the ways of my flesh.

The Distraction of Trauma

Let's take another turn. When we rehearse our past's hurts, pains, and shame as permission to be inconsistently Godly in our today, we pay with our life. Romans 6:23 says *"For the wages of sin is death, but the gift of God is eternal life in[a] Christ Jesus our Lord." NIV*

The enemy's trick is to have us so consumed with what has been done to us(rejection) and through us(guilt) that this allows him to steal the promises of the life that God has gifted to us by making us lose focus and sight of the love and plans of God. Every day that we remain trapped and surrendered to the victim mentality that comes through the repetition of proclaiming the hurt, shame, and fear, instead of proclaiming the good news of God, we are paid by life with the wages of sin, "death."

Now, this death is typically not death, as you may perceive it in a literal way. It manifests itself through being afraid to love and be transparent with others, debt due to the insecurity of self, chronic depression, anxiety, self-sabotage, isolation, poor anger management, and religion instead of relationship. If I missed one, then you fill in your blank _____.

Death is bondage and the inability to freely move as God has designed and paid on the cross for us to do so. Our unwillingness to adhere to the statutes of God (even those pertaining to our worthiness through Christ Jesus) is in fact, a sin that causes us to live as children of darkness and not of light.

Ephesians 5:8 teaches that we were once children of darkness but now we are light so let's live as children of light for this light within us produces only what is good and right and true." It is not that God wants us to ignore our hurts and pains because he says himself in Matthew 11:28-30: *"Come to me, all you who are weary and burdened, and I will give you rest. Take my yoke upon you and learn from me, for I am gentle and humble in heart, and you will find rest for your souls. For my yoke is easy and my burden is light."*

Let me suggest to you that it is not about the pain you've been through but about what you do with your pain and who you trust to give it to. Are you holding up your pain as your badge to not show up as your best self or allowing it to stop you from being vulnerable with God?"

The High Priest who Understands

"For we do not have a high priest who is unable to empathize with our weaknesses, but we have one who has been tempted in every way, just as we are—yet he did not sin."
Hebrews 4:18 AMP

Christ is The High Priest who intercedes on our behalf. He is the lamb that was slain for our sins when He came as Jesus, the Son of God. I would like to believe that beyond needing to die for all of humankind's sins, he was also tempted in all ways possible so that he could have an understanding of what it's like to be us and experience hurt and pain.

From personal experience, and I'm sure you could probably agree, there is no person more comforting while going through a trial than someone else who has experienced the same trial that you are currently suffering. This person can speak and empathize with exactly how you're feeling, exchange stories with you about the matter, and even give you hope for coming out of the situation. I say all of this to introduce you to the God of compassion!

I know in my life the reason why I ran from God so much, never bringing Him my burdens, was because I didn't feel that he wanted the hurt and bruised side of me. I didn't know that imperfection was allowed before such a great God. It wasn't that I didn't honor Him in some way and do my best to exalt him in my life, but I didn't know him as the lover of my soul. I wanted a relationship with Him, and I thought I was doing pretty good within the religious ramifications. However, I had to realize that God didn't want my works and my religious ways; he wanted intimacy with me. I was so used to going through situations (i.e., bullying, divorce, the loss of my mother, and single parenthood, just to name a few) situations in which I would suppress my tears because I thought that was just what adults and Christians did. However, God also wanted the most tender parts of me, those parts that were broken and hurt. He didn't just want them to help me lick my wounds, but He wanted to heal and restore them, and it could only happen if I left the sin of false humility at the door.

Redefining Obedience and Sin

Many times, we wrongly perceive the deeper calling of Jesus as a call to rituals, but on the contrary, it is a call to a rare relationship of honesty and freedom. God wants us to know that we can come to him with our broken hearts. I went to church on Sunday, I paid tithes, and I was a giver; However, God began to show me that I wasn't a giver at all because the one thing that he wanted from me was my heart, and it was closed off in a dark and lonely room with only my past failures, mistakes, and rejection to entertain it.

When God brought this to my attention, this was somewhat of a shattering truth because I saw God as my drill sergeant, requiring me to stay in line, salute him, and do everything just right so that I could receive another promotional rank. I didn't know he called me to be his friend, his beloved, and his daughter. I didn't know the God that wept with Mary and Martha over the death of their brother Lazarus in John 11.

I thought opening up my heart to God was my choice, and it was, but I didn't know that my refusal to be intimate with Jesus was a sin.

The uncovering of this truth led me to the realization that sin is not black and white, it doesn't always have a definitive answer, and mostly it has no look that can be pinpointed; Sin is simply relying on oneself and ignoring the invitations of Christ for intimacy. I didn't know that the ways of sin could reach beyond my pious rituals and manifest in a way in which I handled my pain.

Sin is not a noun; instead, it is a verb that is an act of what you do with the person, place, or thing. We serve a God who knows all about our life's circumstances, and in every situation, we must acknowledge him in all our ways. Acknowledging God in all of our ways consist of us choosing His ways of living and choosing them even in the face of pain, rejection, and hurt.

BEAUTIFYING REJECTION: THE GREAT EXCHANGE

God says in Deuteronomy 30:19 I call heaven and earth to record this day against you, [that] I have set before you life and death, blessing and cursing: therefore, choose life, that both thou and thy seed may live".

Often we do not have a choice over our circumstances, but all the time, we do have a choice over the way we will handle them. The elevation of God only comes through the surrender of our pain to God, and by doing so, we choose the path of life that blesses us, but it also blesses our seed and our lineage.

When we surrender all of us to God, even the aspects of us that we would rather ignore or not acknowledge, we cut off the blood supply of bondage to those areas, thereby destroying the curses of those wounds. Our surrender to God's way sets us free because there is healing in surrendering to the ways of God. This type of healing is only available by way of obedience to the path and vulnerability to God. Being children of the Light means being totally dependent on God's knowledge and the way He has instructed us on how we should live our lives.

To be children of the Light is to practice His ways and allow the Light of Christ to become our identity. It is how we are defined! The old things passed away, and we are made new creatures. As children of the Light, we also realize that we cannot earn the light, but it is instead a gift from our Father. It is not contingent upon our perfect performance in church, work, or our local community. Instead, all good works shall be only the byproduct of the fruits of spirit produced by way of us releasing our dark pain so that we can fully embrace the light of God our Father.

In all of this, we must remember that a big part of humbling ourselves and getting over the distraction of Trauma is acknowledging our feelings as significant but never more significant than the thoughts that God thinks towards us. When we remember this truth, we can also walk with God in humility, being led by His truth and not the Trauma of our past while simultaneously letting God use all that we have been through for His glory.

17

More Than Meets the Eye: Rethinking the Role Of Beauty

For most of my childhood and much of my adulthood, I didn't consider myself as beautiful. In many cases, I would glance over myself and only see scars from the horrible acne I had as a teen, an uneven skin tone, features that were not ideal according to beauty standards, and a waist that just seemed to never fit under a size 16. All I could do was see myself through the eyes of criticism and rejection, so you could probably imagine that my confidence and self-esteem were completely nonexistent.

The constant self-loathing often led me into deep states of depression. I knew that the only way I would come out was to seek wise counsel. So as I began to have an interactive relationship with Christ, I began to learn about what God believed about me. I even began searching for teachings that would affirm and explain what the word of God said, especially about appearance and beauty. Repeatedly, when I heard beauty references, they would be glanced over and somewhat minor in the grand perspective of life.

Most of the time, when I would hear teaching about beauty, many speakers would say something like "God doesn't look at the outside; instead, he looks at the heart" and would leave that explanation there to dismiss personal assessments and questions about beauty as though it didn't matter. Growing up very religious (in the ritual sense), we were even trained that wearing makeup was a sin and that paying attention to such beauty routines was an abomination before God. I've come to learn that sometimes we demonize what we don't know how to explain because it is easier to avoid the scenario altogether than to let down our pride long enough to learn the truth and change directions.

However, even as a young lady, I understood that this train of thought had to be wrong, or the Bible would not consider the mention of appearance and beauty in the scriptures. What I came to realize first was that beauty is not sinful in nature, but just like all other things, the worship of beauty causes idolatry because anything that we allow to stand in place of God is a sin against God. Then, once I understood that, I realized even my self-loathing was a sin against God because I loathe what I thought I lacked; basically, saying that what I thought I lacked in beauty was so important that it would affect my ability to live in my purpose. Anytime anything in life has that kind of hold on you; it is connected to Satan, who is the father of lies because God will always supply you with everything you NEED to be who you are called to be, even your appearance!

As I began to open up my heart so that God could correct my perspective of beauty, I also wanted to understand and debunk even more of the religious rhetoric and cliches I had learned about beauty.

One of the major myths/perspectives I wanted to understand was when others would say, "God doesn't see the outside." I always thought... "How could a God who shaped and crafted me in his own image, gave me fingerprints unlike anyone else, and counts the hairs on my head not see the outside?" Honestly, my personal belief is that this type of explanation only exists because of man's shame of the sin of humanity, possibly even because it is better to think of a God who does not see the outside because then it would be hard

NOT to assign human qualities to Him. But that's a story for another day.

To me, this perspective also uniquely aligns with the disturbing political statement, "I don't see race or color; I only see the person." I understand the intent behind this statement as someone is trying to disarm others about common human biases and solidify that they are not judging anyone. However, this argument generally falls short of an acknowledgment and appreciation for other cultures' natural and God-given differences. The valid point can be made that if a person has to dismiss the God- given qualities of someone to speak to them on a basic level, then instead of disarming the other group of people that they actually confirm that judgment still exists, and their qualities prove to be (at least in their eyes) inaccurate, and even worse, intolerable.

But the Lord said to Samuel, "Do not look at his appearance or at his physical stature, because I have [c]refused him. For[d] the Lord does not see as man sees; for man looks at the outward appearance, but the Lord looks at the heart."
1 Samuel 16:7 NKJV

To understand this scripture, I had to dive deeper into the chapter.

The context of this scripture is within the story where Samuel, a prophet of God, is instructed by God to anoint a new king over Israel after he rejects the current and first king, Saul. In those days, God would send a Prophet to anoint a person to be king over his people, and at this time, God desired the next king to be one of Jesse's sons, but the prophet did not know which one of them. After the preparation (consecration service) of the anointing ceremony had been completed, as all of them would go through a sacred consecration to make themselves clean and acceptable before the Lord's presence, Samuel saw one of Jesse's sons Eliab, and he said: **"Surely the Lord's anointed is before Him!"**. However, this is the moment when God says, **"Do not look at his appearance or at his physical stature, because I have [c]refused him. For[d] the Lord does not see as man sees; for man looks at the outward appearance, but the Lord looks at the heart."**

God spoke this scripture as a prophetic direction to the prophet to keep him focused on the assignment of God and not to use his mindset to do the work of the Lord, for humanity's mindset is not sufficient to do the work of the Lord! Eliab's good-looking appearance was not a sin nor an indication of who He would be; However, in the eyes of the Prophet, it was a distraction from the plan of the Lord. This is an example of how the enemy can use beauty to be a false witness to greatness. However, the mere fact that God could instruct the Prophet to look beyond the appearance of Eliab means God was aware of how great his appearance was.

God's concern for us will always be about our heart, and Eliab's heart was not with God as the next King, and that was the only thing that mattered to God's plan. His gift in appearance was a done deal and given to him at birth, so it would not change, but his heart is what got him disqualified.

In a world full of social media beauty and all things that appear to be glitter and gold, we must remember that even though our appearance may be inspiring, God's number one concern is our heart. Our heart is the piece of us that truly keeps us in a place where we can serve and where God can use us. One of the things that people often say in my community is that "your gifts can get you into a place that your integrity can't keep you in," even as so with beauty. Beauty is a tool that can be used in God's hands, which is why the Bible says he will give us beauty for ashes. However, beauty is only a tool that can get others' attention or even be used to inspire people as with the prophet, but true elevation and addition to your life only comes from God. What I learned during my time of discovery of what beauty meant to me and ultimately what it meant to God was that I should seek his beauty which is found in the heart first, and He would adorn me with the beauty that comes on the outside.

Appearance is a claim; beauty is an advertisement, it gives you a glimpse of what could be true, but it is in the heart where the internal integrity of the person fulfills the promise of what you see on the outside of that person. There is nothing worse than a promise of beauty on the outside but then no beauty to be found on the inside of a person. It is like putting perfume on a dirty body, something sweet on something messy; it simply doesn't mix, and it truly doesn't work for the assignment of God. The transformation that I had as I continued to seek after the Lord was a God-inspired transformation of the heart as my heart transformed so did the outside of me and who I was. We must not esteem beauty as the highest expression of life, although it has its place in our lives and in the world;

we must not esteem it more highly than the heart, rather, they are Co-laborers with each other. Beauty on the outside to serve the heart and the presence of God on the inside of humanity is the ultimate will of God.

18

Knowing Your Value

One day I was lying down on the couch after what was one of the many nights that I hadn't slept. Only to wake up to text messages and more problems to fix, and personal frustration with what my life had become. By this time, I had begun to question why I was even here in life and if I was truly valuable.

Exhausted but unable to go to sleep, I heard God whisper, "Your presence is valuable." If it wasn't for the exhaustion, I would have burst into tears, but at this point, I was unable even to open my eyes. God continued, saying, "Your presence has value, and your presence is missed...I don't tell you this so you can throw around your weight ...I tell you this so you can know your weight".

For many years I went through relationships shutting them down because I felt like the person would be better off without me. Whenever I was confronted, I would discount everything the person said about how hurt they were because I thought it was an act. Thought, "Surely you don't mean it…you're not that hurt" because I thought everyone was lying about how much they valued me. I thought every person in my life who showed me kindness meant that they wanted to use me or found me so pathetic that they were doing me a favor. So, as a result, I thought that I was doing them a favor every time I closed the doors of my heart.

It wasn't them that I hated or didn't like ..most of the time, it was me. I didn't value myself, which led me to not see that closing my space and heart to others was hurtful and harmful to me and others. I didn't value my relationships, and it wasn't because I didn't value the people, in fact, I probably overvalued the people, which is idolatry (a sin). I didn't value the relationships because I felt that I was too inadequate to have them in the first place. I lived on an internal belief system that I was unworthy of love and acceptance. Therefore, I lived under the limiting belief that caused me to act as such.

My life shifted at the point when I heard the Lord say, **"…Know your weight."**

Spiritually, every soul that God created has weight. Weight is the essence, the personality, the desires, the love, the ideas, the dreams, and the uniqueness of a person.

Our souls are the only part of us that goes back to God when we expire in the earthly realm because that's how valuable our souls are. Jesus literally came to save our souls and put us in the right standing with the Father because that's how valuable the soul of man is to him. The soul is the glory factor of God wrapped up inside of our body. That said, it is the most valuable entity in our life and the life of others. It is where our creativity and empathy for other soul's flow from.

Every time we enter someone's life, we are bringing all of these valuable attributes of us with us to them, and every time we leave, we take them with us. Whether or not you or they value what you have, it is more valuable than anything that can be evaluated.

Even more than that, no one has the power to value or devalue your soul and its expressions, not even your own self.

In a world that constantly tries to tell you who you are, God wants you to know the weight and value that He has deposited into you. The reason why God wants you to know your weight is because He knows that your evolution into a better you begins at the place of how you value yourself. We will talk more about finding your value in the coming chapters.

Prayer:

God, I pray that you show me the value you have deposited into me. Help me to see beyond the world and my critiques of myself into the mysteries of why you even created me. Help me to absorb my value from You and not from Men in Jesus' name. Amen.

19

Fortifying the New You: Resisting Life's Contradictions

Every year, my social media timelines are filled with the promotional collateral of so many motivational conferences, and the number of conferences seems to be growing daily. Even during the pandemic, I feel like I saw more flyers for virtual conferences than I had ever seen in my life! If that is not enough, our culture is constantly bombarded with virtual seminars, podcasts, and live videos based solely on motivating others.

I couldn't help but think about the phenomenon of motivation culture that is continuing to rise and soar and how people spend thousands on thousands to engage in the motivation factor. In all transparency, I, too, can remember a time when all I would do was search for motivational videos, countless speeches, and nonstop sermons. Even more interesting, I would particularly search for motivation after I received a word from God. I noticed I had a pattern:

1. Get a word or uncommon revelation,
2. Worship
3. Go on to try and get motivated to do (blank)
4. Get motivated and do alittle work
5. Then loose motivation and never finish

I didn't realize that when I searched for motivation, what I was actually seeking for was to keep the word that God spoke over my heart alive. I spent so much money, time, and energy trying to be motivated until God confronted me on this point. I found that the search in my heart to feel motivated was nothing more than the dream in me asking to live but the skeptic in me that kept looking for proof that it could live.

Listen, I'm just going to come out of the gate and say that the word of God on your life doesn't need permission for what God has already ordained to be manifested in your life. The word of God says, " I will do a new thing" in you "shall you not know it?" (Isaiah 43:19)

If God wants to do something new through us, then why do we run to motivation to see if it can be done? My brother and sister... the permission is in your walking!

When we search for motivation, we subject and surrender our dreams, visions, and destiny to the limited resource of motivation, which does not have the capacity nor the ability to fulfill the vision. With all due respect to your favorite speaker, teacher, preacher, prophet, mentor, coach, televangelist, sister, brother, auntie, and Momma... no matter what your motivator says whether good or bad, it will never be strong enough to accomplish what God gave you to accomplish.

Who He has called you to be is not produced out of what you feel like; it's produced out of your obedience to walk in who God already says you are. When God gives you instructions, He does not need your feelings to cooperate. He needs your obedience to operate. However, in our humanness, we tend to try and wait until we feel MOTIVATED to move on to what God has given us to do, which is why we can sometimes continually walk in circles searching for motivation because we are seeking for confirmation.

Perhaps you are not where you thought you would be, or you feel like you might have heard the Lord but you aren't sure and need confirmation. I was there where you sit, and I felt the same way. However, what I had to learn first and what I want to share with you is that when God gave you a vision, he gave it to YOU for a reason. There is a reason why we have vision and revelation of the destiny on our lives, and I believe it's because God knew that nothing around us would look like what it shall be in the end. Who you are becoming is night and day to who you are right now! The Bible says in Habakkuk 2:2:

2 Then the LORD replied:
"Write down the revelation and make it plain on tablets so that a herald[b] may run with it. 3 For the revelation awaits an appointed time it speaks of the end and will not prove false. Though it linger, wait for it; it[c] will certainly come and will not delay.

Specifically, I would like to lean in on "Though it lingers, wait for it..."! If you are anything like me, typically when you get a revelation about what God has for you or who He is making you to be, you get super excited. Especially if you've received this revelation or vision through someone else spontaneously, it feels like it connects with every fiber of your being and draws you into a passionate experience of hope and drive. A little after this happens, you may take a little time to ponder over this and imagine what this means for you and your family, which makes you super pumped to see this happen!

Then after, you soon return back to your daily task and routines, still beaming with excitement because of the experience. As time goes on, you think about it every day and may even go back to review what you wrote or play it back in your mind, but life keeps playing the same as before. In zeal, you may even choose to share it with a friend or family member who may say, "Good for you or at em, girl," and then you silently think to yourself I guess it's not that big of a deal or either I must be crazy to think that this will happen.

Little, by little, by little...you remember it, but since there is nothing around you that confirms it, you kind of store it away. This leaves you without the ability to get up and press forward, and before you know it... we're trying to get to the next conference so we can feel a shot of destiny and motivation to move.

Friends, this is not the life God has called us to, constantly looking for more and more words of affirmation. There comes a time when we must stand on the word that we have already received. We keep that prophecy alive by revisiting it and in the face of uncertainty, choosing not to waver no matter the oxymoron that exists between the prophecy over our life versus our current life situation.

Specifically, when we reach a hard patch of life that appears to be in contradiction to what God has promised us, instead of putting down the word or prophecy, we must choose to pick it up and bring it before God. Many times, I will even bring it to God and ask Him to remind me and reinforce the Word in my life afresh. We must be aware that this new revelation of who we are will be fought by life and even those who would prefer the person we were when we were in the bondage of rejection versus the free us. It now becomes our responsibility to ask God to help us to keep the word He gave us.

Another thing we must recognize is that there is a difference between guarding the revelation versus trying to make it happen in our own strength.

The LORD said to me, "You have seen correctly, for I am watching to see that my word is fulfilled."
Jeremiah 1:12, NIV

Who God reveals to you that you are is who you are becoming, so it is not about you making it happen; it is about you being in the posture of the belief that you can be who God says you are, and by being in the posture He then transforms you into that person. I said that to say that keeping the revelation of you alive means that you stay connected to the word no matter what, while also acknowledging that God is the overseer of its fulfillment in you. This is simply about not being your own stumbling block that stops you from moving forward in your life.

My prayer for you today is that you will know that the revelation that God has given you about your identity is enough and that you stay connected to what God has decreed into you no matter the circumstance you find yourself in!

20

From Residue to Restoration: Believing in the Remnants

Wake up and strengthen all that remains...
Revelation 3:2 NIV

Rejection has a way of having us constantly reminisce on our pain. It joins with fear and can cause us to constantly reference back to other situations in our lives that are similar to the current circumstance to keep us safe (air quotes) from the same heartbreak that we previously experienced. Through my own experiences and the opportunity of watching others, I can say that when we run into moments that feel like what we felt at another time, it can trigger the part of us that remembers what it felt like to be rejected or ostracized.

For years of my life, I lived in a constant state of overanalyzing the people around me and their intentions. People would complement me, and I would quickly dismiss all the nice things said about me. Other times, I would take my close friends through the wringer to see if they were really my friends and cared about me like they said they did.

Even my love life suffered because I would only let someone get so close before pushing them away or trying to subconsciously start a fight or disagreement to prove that we weren't compatible. I would literally opt out of dating or social events because I couldn't handle the anxiety and threat of depression that the possibility of rejection held over my head. Just the thought of facing another rejection like I had in childhood would send me into a spiral thought process of what-ifs and false scenarios that I had no room for.

As if this wasn't enough, I constantly pondered over the thoughts of what I had lost (time, relationships, experiences) and why it kept me from moving forward in healing. Due to my undiagnosed PTSD(self-proclaimed) from childhood bullying, when I got to a certain age, I realized that I had lost so many experiences and relationships that could have worked. Of course, I wanted to be healed, but I hadn't yet come to the place of acknowledging that the process of healing was a part of the healing experience as well. In reality, part of healing and moving on with life is accepting the number of times you have even tried to get to the point of healing.

I became indifferent because I was walking with a newfound confidence that I wished I would have had years ago! I wished that I believed in myself at 18 as I believed in myself at 32. I wish I felt as beautiful at 14 as I did at 28. I wish I had learned that people's opinions of me didn't matter, as I learned at 29.

It's so crazy because I felt like I had lost so much time and energy on unnecessary things, moments, and people. So much so that I had begun to believe that accepting healing at this age wouldn't mean anything anymore; I knew that rejection and fear were a thief, but sometimes what we "think" we know can be our worst enemy. I thought that what I could have had was a done deal. I knew I couldn't get my 20s back…like they were gone, and it was my fault for allowing myself to be duked out of those relationships and occasions for fun and connection.

However, God spoke to me and said, "Strengthen what remains." God knew my little, smart-mouth, stubborn self didn't want to walk through the process because I didn't feel that it mattered anymore. I felt like everything wrong had already happened, and it wasn't reversible:

_Divorce
_Solo Mom hood
_Went to college and graduated late with no job prospects.
_Loss of countless relationships
_Loss of opportunities because I did not feel sufficient.
Shall I go on?

I knew my soul needed healing so that I could live in peace and treat others like Christ would want me to, but I still felt like I had missed out on everything! So why even go through strengthening or transforming anything now?

God spoke and said, "Bianca, I know you believe in me, but it hurts that you don't believe in you. It hurts me as your Father to know that you don't believe in the YOU that I created you to be. I don't just want you to love me and worship me, and you never see and love the piece of me that I put in you."

There is an aspect of the Father that God put in all of us to be sweetly expressed in this world in such a way that only it could be expressed through us. The beauty of God combined with the expressions of our personality, wit, and flavor gives off a sweet aroma in this earth that creates a beautiful aroma in the nostrils of God and sparks joy in the hearts of men that opinions can't contain. However, this set harmony cannot take place by participation only; it must be a byproduct and overflow of our belief and commitment to be living epistles.

To *participate* and to *commit* are two very different things. When we participate, we simply take part in an action or endeavor but when we commit to something we pledge and devote ourselves to the mission. When we participate, our focus is on us and the fact that we are going along with the program but when we commit, we recognize that the actions are to serve a greater purpose. In a commitment it is no longer about the action but more so about the completed mission.

God was asking me to stop being a participant in his program...He now called me higher to become a *Committed one*.

Years ago, I used to say it doesn't matter what my choice is because God is strong enough to drag me anyway. As I grew, I realized that God was calling me into a covenant, which is an agreement between two parties. I would often hear how God wanted to bless me and give me a life of abundance, and I could never figure out why it was not happening. I came to realize that it wasn't happening because I still wanted God to drag me into obedience and success. That thought worked for the season I was in at the time, but I realized that the theory of God *"dragging me"* was all wrong.

First of all, why would anyone want someone else to drag them anywhere? Even more so, why would anyone want to be the one dragging someone else somewhere?

I know firsthand the frustration of being a parent who has to drag a kid to a store when they don't want to go. As a matter of fact, when my son got to a certain age, I would ask family members to watch him at their house just to have a peaceful walk in the store without him asking, "When are we leaving?" or "Why do we have to be here"... or even worse the complaint, "MY FEET HURT"....UGH the stress is real. I just wanted to let him stay with a family member because I didn't want to hear it, not just because it was overwhelming but because it also would make me feel like a bad parent for bringing my son along when he didn't want to be there.

I had to realize that if this was my truth, then could it not be true that God felt the same way?

When I was a child, I spoke as a child, I understood as a child, I thought as a child; but when I became a man, I put away childish things...
1 Corinthians 13:11

It was time to move from God dragging me along in purpose to choosing to be committed. It was time to put away the childish behavior! Children are pulled, but adults are asked! God wanted me to become his partner in great works, not his slave to be dragged! The Bible says that we are joint heirs...meaning that by God's grace, we share the inheritance. The problem comes in when we don't truly believe or see ourselves as the joint heirs of a king, so we end up acting more like slaves than partners in the work of God.

Naturally, every parent wants their child to believe in themselves and cherish who they were created to be.

We want them to love themselves because if they love themselves, then we know that they won't look for validation in the treacherous streets of life. Every great parent knows that raising our kids to value themselves and love how the Lord created them will lead to them making better choices!

We have to understand that a big part of loving the Father is also seeing and treasuring the value that he has placed in us. When we see this, then we know that nothing in life is truly lost if we have breath in our body. We also know that nothing we have been through can stop us from wanting to be and live the best life that God has for us, even if we feel like it is coming later in life than we planned.

> *"So I will restore to you the years that the*
> *swarming [a]locust has eaten,*
> *The crawling locust,*
> *The consuming locust,*
> *And the chewing locust,*
> *My great army which I sent among you.*
> *You shall eat in plenty and be satisfied,*
> *And praise the name of the Lord your God,*
> *Who has dealt wondrously with you;*
> *And My people shall never be put to shame. Then you*

> *shall know that I am in the midst of Israel:*
> *I am the Lord your God*
> *And there is no other.*
> *My people shall never be put to shame.,"*
> *Joel 2:25-27, NKJV*

God's word even says that He will restore the years the enemy stole! In short, nothing that years of pain and rejection took from us can stop the restoration of what God will do for us if we believe and trust in him! When God said, "Strengthen what remains," he was saying to value what we have now and treat it well. We must be careful not to let our past hurts tell us who we shouldn't try to become now!

God wanted me to become his partner in great works, not his slave, and I believe that's what He wants for you, too. I believe he wants us as his partners because that's just how much he believes in us.

He believes in us so much that he sent the Son to be the ransom for our sins so that we can have eternal life.

He believes in us so much that he decided to place his beautiful heavenly treasures in us. He believes in us so much that He is willing to put everything on the line just to give us the opportunity to be a part of his plan and will for the entire world.

On my phone, as my screen saver, I have a quote from an unknown source that I look at every day that I would like to share with you to ponder over. God has continued to confirm this quote to me every day, and I pray that He will do the same for you. I encourage you to write this quote out on a sticky note or type it on your phone for safekeeping to review when you come across days that seem to bring you low.

"Rest in this, God believes in you more than you believe in yourself." Let this quote bring you comfort because the God of everything perfect and beautiful is your biggest cheerleader, so how could you doubt yourself?

What shall we then say to these things? If God be for us, who can be against us?
Romans 8:31 NKJV

21

Borrowed Belief

One night, I sat in my room after being frustrated the whole day and just overwhelmed. I literally said out loud, "God, I don't want to go on another fast, give another offering into the collection plate, read another scripture, and break it down into the Hebrew, nor consecrate myself God...not because I believe they don't work but because I no longer believe in me."

I would never dare to say that the principles I have been taught in my Bible and through great teaching and preaching are ineffective. I'd seen God do many wonders in my life and the life of others. I knew that God was a miracle-working, healing, and delivering God. I knew that God, the one who sent Jesus to the cross to bear the sins of the world, was perfect always and in all of his ways! I knew that his ways were so great that they were above my ways! I believed that if he said he would do something, then he would make it happen! In the words of my great-aunt, Elnora, "He's never short of his word." I believed in Him, the *Great I AM*, the Alpha and Omega (beginning and the end), and all that He encompassed. It was ME that I no longer believed in!

There was a time when I looked around my life, and nothing looked like God loved me at all. In fact, I kept apologizing to God because I felt like "I must have done something wrong to end up here." Here I am, raising a kid alone, without a regular job, barely scraping by in my business, not to mention all of the mental battles of depression and thoughts of suicide that visited my bedside frequently. I remember reexamining my life over and over to see what I had done to pull this on myself. As a mother, I tried to marry my son's father, which ended up in a terrible heartbreak and divorce, leaving me to become a solo full-time mother. As a young lady trying to pick up the pieces, I listened to the voice of the Lord when God told me to go to college, and I went, excelled, and graduated with honors. As a young lady, I gave my life over to the Lord and got super involved in church, choir director, praise and worship team leader, ministry assistant, media ministry, you name it, and I was there; I even took my tithing very seriously. I wasn't perfect in my relationships, but I sure did try, and I was very quick to apologize, even if I felt the slightest bit of offense on my end or the opposite.

After looking at all of that, I then started searching because I thought "maybe I'm not doing enough". I began to take more spiritual courses online and tried to fast (notice I said tried, lol). As a matter of fact, I became a vegetarian for almost three years. Now, I'd be lying if I said that I saw no improvement, but I could still say that there was not a huge shift. All the while, God kept prophesying to me through dreams, visions, and people. I was getting words about stages & platforms, ministry, business, and wealth. While I was in some of my darkest days where all I wanted to do was check out of life, people would come and say, "God said you are exactly where you are supposed to be,"... "God has big plans for your life."

Now, don't get me wrong, it always felt good to get a word from God about my future because it felt like a warm hug from the father as he whispered in my ear,

"I haven't forgotten about you,"...and even more " You are still on the right track." Boy, did that help me!

But after a while, I would be discouraged again and back in that space of trying to figure out what I was doing wrong. Many days, I cried because I couldn't understand why God would tell me so many great things and encourage my heart, but yet I felt that I could never get there. After so long, the things I would normally do, like read my Bible, worship, pray, and fast, began to feel like chores...not because they were not good, but I just didn't believe that I was doing them right and if I wasn't getting it right and my life still ended up terrible, then I thought "what was the point of even trying?"

(don't you dare walk away from this book now...there is a revelation beyond your pain...keep reading)

As a result of me not continually engaging in what was meant to nourish my soul, I would really be depleted and even more frustrated and hurt. I looked around and saw God blessing others and felt like the blessing on them was God's rejection of me. It pretty much reinforced my belief that I was not good enough to receive God's blessings for me. I honestly just felt that

I was a reject in the eyesight of God and that what I was going through in life was rightfully due to me because of how terrible I was as Christ's daughter.

Did I mention that during all of this, I was still serving in ministry, actually being used by God to prophesy in the lives of people, being given opportunities to work with people on large platforms, and even being interviewed?

I would study enough to sow a word in the hearts of God's people, say a prayer over other people in the name of Jesus, and they would receive blessings and miracles. I literally had one friend that I prayed with on a private matter call me a couple of weeks later and say, "After you prayed with me, immediately things started opening up for me"… she said that she asked God, "I wonder if she [Me] knows that her prayers work that fast?"

The answer is, "I didn't have a clue" While I was watching others that I prayed with and for prospering in God's promises, I stood back and felt like the imposter in the room. Always thinking, "Oh no, someone is going to see that I am pretending and that I am not truly blessed." You see I knew that I was called by God, but I didn't believe that I reflected, represented, nor could stand up to the calling of God on my life.

The constant torment of this belief system had become so dysfunctionally ingrained into my way of thinking that even when I prayed, I would never pray for myself other than asking for forgiveness and help to stop doing things wrong. I would be afraid to spend time alone with God in silence because I was afraid that something else wrong with me would be highlighted. By the end of this time, I was so beaten up spiritually that I just couldn't take any more beatings because I felt I had no more fight in me.

This led me to the night sitting in my room saying, "No more considerations, no more fast, JUST NO MORE" because I felt as if it hadn't changed me enough to the point that I would finally be able to take care of my son which felt so small in comparison to what I knew about what God could do, then why keep trying to believe, dream, and imagine?

Now I know that this is generally the point in a story when the skies open and the hero comes swooping in to save the damsel in distress, which would have been me.

Butttt.... I'm sorry, I must burst your bubble because this didn't happen (stay tuned, it might one day as the story is still being written). However, something much more interesting did.

Sitting in that very same spot, God began to bring back to me a Bible story that echoed throughout that season in my life from the book of 2 Kings, chapter 4. This story is really cool and has a large amount of meaning in many different respects, but specifically, there is one part that jumped out at me during that time.

For those who don't know this story, the Prophet Elisha is with a woman who had recently become a widow who comes to him in distress because her late husband owed debt collectors before he died, and the creditors are now coming after her family. She goes to the Prophet because her husband was once a servant of his, and she doesn't have a clue of what to do. Elisha hears out her problem and then asks her what she has in her house, and she says, "nothing except a little oil" he then advises her to go and borrow as many jars as she can from all of her neighbors and then use the oil in her house to fill them up and sell them to pay off debts and live off the rest of what's left.

There are so many moving parts that we could discuss, such as the oil, which I equate to the anointing, gifts, talent, and skills that she possessed, and also how she viewed it as ONLY a little, which speaks to her devaluing what's in her own house. Or we can also speak about how oil as a substance only needs to be used a little bit because it is so thick and heavy in its flow, which speaks to how whatever she has is so potent that it only takes a little bit in the first place.

However, my attention was drawn to the jars or pots that she had to borrow. I find it interesting that she had the substances to flow but not the containment or the capacity! You see, we could have all the right stuff to attain the blessing but not the containment or the capacity to receive the flow of God's blessings properly. Everything was in her house: the oil and the labor but not the capacity.

Capacity can be defined as the potential or suitability for holding, storing, or accommodating. Also, an individual's mental or physical ability"
(Merriam-Webster.com)

As long as she didn't believe she had anything, there was no solution to her debt. Say this out loud "**BELIEF CREATES CAPACITY TO RECEIVE.**"

Our belief causes us to see answers instead of problems. Belief opens our YES up to see with a God kind of perception which is exactly what the prophet Elisha had. He heard a problem and found a solution in "the little" bit because he believed that it was enough even when she did not. However, based on her belief in him, she was obedient to his instructions and reaped a harvest.

As I sat in the chair, reminiscing on this Bible story, I began to realize why she had to go to borrow the pots from others, and that's because she had to borrow their belief.

The reason why her neighbors had so many jars is that they believed they had a need for them and that their jars would once be full. Her neighbors were stocking up capacity for their own overflow. I always found it interesting that she didn't have any jars when it seemed that she should have if she had nothing, but she was at a place where she didn't even expect flow and blessing anymore.

Kind of sounded like me…

I began to open my mouth and speak very softly so as not to wake up the family, "Lord, can I borrow some of your belief?". I believe in you, but I don't believe in me…I no longer believe that what's in this house, in this vessel, in this mind that what I have is enough…Can I borrow some of your belief?"

Then God said to me, "The blessings that you see on others is what stretches your capacity to believe again."

Friend, if you are in a dry season and it seems like everyone else around you is in God's flow and getting it, then I want you to know that by you seeing the flow of others is God's invitation for you to receive your own flow and believe again.

I have come to realize that in life, we will not always believe in ourselves. Being in Christ Jesus is very simple, but being a Human being is messy and can get very complicated. Even Paul said, "Lord, I believe but help my unbelief," and believe it or not, that is the good news! We have a Lord and Savior who can help the unbelief in us, the part that would stop our flow and outpouring, the aspect of us that loves God with our whole heart yet dislikes or finds ourselves unworthy.

God knows about the areas of us that don't quite fully believe or feel weak from the constant hardships of life. However, once we discover this place of unbelief, it is now time to go to the Father "who will withhold no good thing from us" (Psalms 84:11), and ask him for help in that area. God is not trying to torment you by showing you the great things He is doing for others, He is just stretching your capacity to believe for yourself.

Pray this prayer with me: *Father, thank you for highlighting the areas in me that may be worn down because of the constant Ebbs and flows of this world. Lord, I pray that you forgive me for any disobediences that has resulted from my lack of belief in you or me. I ask that you cover my mind so that I think your heavenly thoughts. I pray that if there is anything in my mindset and ways that do not line up with your promises over my life that you would uproot them and replace them with your thoughts, plans, structures, and good news. I* *decree and declare that every place of lack resulting from the unbelief in my heart is dismantled, and my belief, capacity, and containment are enlarging even as I speak this prayer. I surrender to God's perfect plan now, and I commit to doing so even in the moments when God's instructions make no logical sense. Have your complete way in my life Jesus. Thank you, Lord. In the name of Jesus. Amen.*

22

From False Foundations to Solid Ground: The Journey from Misplaced to Anchored Confidence

Mistaken Identity

The story of the prodigal son is one of the parables that has always been super interesting to me. This parable starts in the Bible by saying there was a man with two sons, one older and one younger. Then, the story proceeds to share with us that the younger son goes to his father and asks him for the portion of his inheritance. Now, I have never had the opportunity to have a father or mother with an inheritance, but from what I understand, an inheritance is not allocated to the recipients until the party who owns the wealth dies. So, for this young man to go to his father and ask for his portion of the inheritance says two things.

The first thing that it says is that He is seriously confused about the point of inheritance. The second thing that it says is that He had no honor for His father, only for his father's wealth, to the point that his father's death is a commodity of gain for his selfish desires.

The prodigal son was more connected to his father's possession than the actual relationship with his father; therefore, this son's confidence was in what his father had materialistically, not what He received relationally. He seemingly built his own confidence on the back of possessions, which is why he asked for the inheritance and then went away to pursue his own desires with his father's belongings, yet without his father. For years, I looked at the prodigal son story and only saw a selfish, self-absorbed, spoiled child until God opened my eyes to the prodigal child within me.

On a closer look, the prodigal son was not just money-hungry; he was also hungry to find himself, and He thought that He could find himself in the wealth of his father's riches. The Bible says that after the father gave the young son his portion, the young man went off and squandered his riches "in wild living."

Looking over my life, I can see a correlation between me and the prodigal son. There were times when I thought, "Jesus, if you just bless me with this, then I would be made whole." Sometimes, I would just daydream about a day when I would have the blessings of the Lord and how I would be able to live life in freedom. In my heart, I built up my hopes and based my future on getting what I wanted. I put my identity into what I would have rather than allowed my identity to be based on the fact that I was the daughter of The King above all Kings.

Ultimately, I learned that when we don't have confidence in the Father, we can misplace our confidence and put it in things. The prodigal son had confidence in what his father had, not in the fact that He was the son of a great man.

To some degree, I also think that the prodigal son could have wanted to be as liberating and kingly as his father was. I believe that he thought if he had what his father had, then he would be who his father was, he would do what he thought his father did, and he would have the friends and everything that he ever wanted. However, the story shows that He did not end up where He thought He would.

"Not long after that, the younger son got together all he had, set off for a distant country and there squandered his wealth in wild living. After he had spent everything, there was a severe famine in that whole country, and he began to be in need. So he went and hired himself out to a citizen of that country, who sent him to his fields to feed pigs. He longed to fill his stomach with the pods that the pigs were eating, but no one gave him anything."

_Luke 15:13-16, NIV

The story says that after all of that "wild living," that a famine came over the land, and He began to come into need and had to, in layman's terms, get a job. Anytime we misplace our trust in God and exchange relationship with Him for things, we will always find ourselves in a depleted state because to take the gifts of God in exchange for our relationship with him is to cut ourselves off from the vine. It is like taking an apple from an apple tree and leaving. We may be full for a while because the apple can nourish us now, but the tree has both the power to nourish and replenish its supply.

The problem of the prodigal son is that he disconnected from the vine that produced the wealth; he got his father's produce, but he lost the connection with his father, not realizing that it was the connection that made the blessings come forth and remain. Everything we need to be fruitful is in the connection to Jesus because the connection to the vine keeps us alive, replenished, and living in abundance. The prodigal son had to learn this lesson the hard way.

16 He longed to fill his stomach with the pods that the pigs were eating, but no one gave him anything. 17 "When he came to his senses, he said, 'How many of my father's hired servants have food to spare, and here I am starving to death! 18 I will set out and go back to my father and say to him: Father, I have sinned against heaven and against you. 19 I am no longer worthy to be called your son; make me like one of your hired servants.' 20 So he got up and went to his father. (NIV)

The Bible goes on to say that He whelmed up in a hog pen, realizing that He had nothing because He had squandered everything. Have you ever been in a place where you looked over at everything you had, only to come to a place and have nothing? Have you ever hit rock bottom so hard that your life wasn't even recognizable anymore? That's a tough place!

That place is so tough that you could even start thinking that the place of filth is where you belong. As a previously known prodigal daughter, I can testify that I am familiar with the hog pin that the prodigal son sat in. I know what it's like to sit in a mess that I created but weighted down with shame, guilt, and defeat with no one else to blame but myself. If we are not careful, this place can be even more lethal than the sin that proceeds this place because the Hog pin is the place that tries to trick us into identifying ourselves by our circumstances. The Hog pin whispers to us how much of a screw-up we are and tries to make a fool of us. It is a lethal place because, unfortunately, this is the place where many people's stories end because since they mistook their identity with things and put their confidence in material items, then the lack thereof and poverty of their current situations becomes a reminder of what they feel they lack and a testament against who they would like to be.

The prodigal son in this story must have begun to feel a type of way about himself in that filthy place. The

Bible says, "he came to himself," and that phrase is the place where I want us to stick a thumbtack.

What is coming to ourselves?

"And when he came to himself, he said, How many hired servants of my father's have bread enough and to spare, and I perish with hunger! I will arise and go to my father, and will say unto him, Father, I have sinned against heaven, and before thee…"
Luke 15:17-18 ESV

If the prodigal son came to himself, then that must mean that before that moment, He must have been living as someone else. I believe the reference to him coming to himself acknowledges the spirit that He allowed to operate within him prior to that moment in the presence of his ability to make another choice and choose his Kingly character.

Our choices and the spirit in which we make them can lead us to an unrecognizable place. However, when we are in that place of filth where everything is covered in the ashes of our poor choices and the rejection of others, we must remember that no matter how bad it looks, our identity in Christ never expires!

Even in our darkest moments of despair and even when we have rejected God, God never takes the opportunity away for us to come home to him as his child. It's all a matter of choosing to step into the sonship identity of Christ.

The Divine Connection

The Bible says he came to himself, and to me, it sounds like he came to his connection with his father and his royal lineage.

"...How many hired servants of my father's have bread enough and to spare, and I perish with hunger! I will arise and go to my father, and will say unto him, Father, I have sinned against heaven, and before thee..."
Luke 15:17-18 (cont.)

Before the prodigal son ran off with his inheritance, it was about what his father had, but after coming to himself, He essentially evaluates where He is in the filth, starving and perishing while even his father's servants are doing better than He is at the present moment.

It's as though he is saying to himself that even if my father does not accept me as a son, He will at least accept me as a servant. The prodigal son knew he was called to be more and better than where he currently was.

Sidebar: It is better to live in humble means in the house of the Lord than to live a life of luxury outside of the house of God.

Rightly placed confidence

The problem with the prodigal son, in the beginning, was that he put his confidence in things instead of His connection with His father, He didn't realize that the connection to His father is what gave him access to the quality of life He had and similarly, when we don't appreciate and acknowledge the connection with God as more valuable than things, then we find ourselves in lost places such as the prodigal son.

"For those who exalt themselves will be humbled, and those who humble themselves will be exalted."
Matthew 23:12 NIV

Unfortunately, the prodigal son elevated himself by asking for an early inheritance, and anytime we exalt ourselves, God will humble us by bringing us down (for our own good). When we rely on the things we can acquire in this world for our confidence and status, we end up losing out in the end. However, the true confidence we should rely on is the confidence in the connection with Jesus.

This is not the kind of confidence that comes from a false humility place of saying that we are nobodies just sharing about Jesus. God says that you are more precious than rubies, the apple of His eyes, and His workmanship, so how can we, in turn, be a nobody? The truth of the matter is that we are somebody because we are connected to the great I AM.

My mentor Dee said something to me while I was in college that I will never forget. Dee said, "When you get to a certain place with God, He don't connect you with slop or just anybody." I believe that as the prodigal son began to come to himself through the connection of His father, he realized that where he was at the time was not of the connection of God. When we realize that our value comes from our God-connection, then the things of this world have no power over us to make us anxious for them, and not only that, but we discover our true value and identity. Anytime we put our value outside of God, we have put it in shaky and fleeting territory that cannot sustain us, but when we find value in our Christ connection, we can be sure that on Christ the solid rock we can stand!

When we get to the place where we rest, rely, and are confident in the fact that we are connected to the Almighty God, then we tap into a divine access of reward.

> *"So do not throw away this confident trust in the Lord. Remember the great reward it brings you!"*
> *Hebrews 10:35 NLT*

God says in His word that He wants us to put our confidence in him.

The definition of confidence means *to trust and know that something or someone is reliable.*

The way that we remain grounded and sturdy in confidence is when we believe and trust that God is reliable. God has made many promises to us, but due to our situations, it can seem that the promises may not happen because our environment (and even who we are presently) isn't conducive to producing the promise.

The Bible does not say what prompted the younger son to ask for his inheritance early, but I believe that He became so impatient because maybe He thought it wouldn't happen and got frustrated in the waiting period. As bad as this sounds, I believe He said to himself, this man is healthy and will live a long time; I won't ever get it. Many people get discouraged in the place of waiting and unfortunately, focus on how far their situation is from looking like the promise and forget all about The One who made the promise in the first place.

However, we cannot let our situations make us throw away our confidence because our confidence and hope was never meant to be in our situation; it was only meant to be in God! In those times when we feel shaken, we must remember these things...

1. God is reliable.
2. Our relationship with God is reliable.
3. Our relationship with God is necessary.

Our relationship with God is our confidence that we will be and become all that God has promised us we would be. We must remember that God is making us into who we need to be to handle what He has prepared for us. The truth is that the waiting period was necessary for the prodigal's son's development, but because he went ahead of his timing, we see that he lost everything due to his immaturity. Misplaced confidence can cause us to get out of God's divine order, but I decree and declare that you are coming into full alignment with placing your confidence in God!

Prayer: Father, I thank you that I can place my confidence in you! Help me stay in the development of your divine order so that I do not put my confidence in worldly things but that it will remain in your statutes. In Jesus' name. Amen.

23

The Lavish Life Redefined

When I say the word lavish, what comes to mind?

I can tell you what comes to mind for me. Now, I am about to date myself a bit here, but when I hear the word lavish, I think about the classic MTV shows, like "Pimp My Ride," that had TV screens in the back of the headrest in cars. Then I think about the MTV show Cribs and the luxurious lifestyles of the wealthy, the rich, and the influential. I think about their parties and how they socialize, or how they travel all the way to another country for a nice cup of coffee, or maybe even their plastic surgeons and their many misuses, chefs, gold, and even emeralds.

I think about everything that glitters, but many of us know that everything that glitters is not gold! As a young girl growing up with the accessibility to MTV and VH1 and all of these other platform that floated around the visuals of a wealthy and luxurious lifestyle, it seemed like the ultimate lavish life. Even the magazines that had cover girls with perfect slim bodies completed with well-proportioned hips-to-bust ratios. I grew up idolizing these people and their life of luxury, even though I never knew that their plastic surgeons were giving them the "perfect" shape and esthetic. Nevertheless, with smooth skin and pretty teeth, nice cars, and a nice house, it all seemed like the ultimate life. I just knew that these people had something that I did not, and it was dreamy, but most of all, it was lavish.

So, to my surprise when God began to speak to me about wanting to give me a lavish lifestyle, I couldn't help but think about some of those things. I began to say to myself:

" Please give me a break. Maybe I'm just imagining that God is saying a lavish lifestyle.
How can I obtain any of that?
And should I even be pursuing it in the first place? Do I even look the part?
Would I fit in with the group of people who were as beautiful, talented, and as rich as the many people I saw living a lavish lifestyle?"

My mind completely ran away with it, but when God speaks, I have now learned that any word and anything he says has no roots in vanity, and it's nothing like what we expect it to be according to human and men's standards. A lavish lifestyle in 1 John 3:1 in the Bible says,

"See what great love the Father has lavished on us, that we should be called children of God! And that is what we are! The reason the world does not know us is that it did not know him." NIV

This is a remarkably interesting choice of words in reference to how the word of God references the Father's *lavishness* of love that He has for us! God was speaking about his lavish love because God's love contains so much that it cannot be confined by one attribute.

His love is so potent.
His love is so unique.
His love is so needed.
His love is so rare that he would have to give it away because no one could afford to pay for it.

You see, God's love is not a thing that we can purchase. It's not a thing that we can buy or that we can find or even really travel for.

God's love is exclusive, and the only way that we can get it is by receiving it from God through relationship with Him.

When God began to speak about the lavish lifestyle, I believe he was saying to live in a way that acknowledged His lavish love for us. I believe His love is unlike anything that we've ever seen before. His love is so rare that not even our mothers, our fathers, our sisters, our brothers, our children, our best friend, our husband or wife, nothing, no *ONE* creation could ever give us the expensive and rare love that Jesus Christ has lavished on us.

What I find so beautiful about the love of God is that He is so willing to make his lavish love accessible to all of us. He spares no expense when giving it to us because God runs out of nothing.

If you are anything like me, you know what it's like to experience the moment when someone's love runs out for you. You have experienced someone's tolerance worn out for you. You have experienced what it feels like for someone to love you one moment, give you a little bit of themselves, and then, all at one time, completely reject you or abandon you the next. Maybe they might have stop talking to you as if you all never knew each other intimately, whether in a romantic relationship, a friendship, or your kindred. We've all experienced moments where seemingly the love we thought would last forever and a lifetime ended in a split moment.

I recently watched a talk show where the host gave a lot of great consultative advice. I won't mention the name of the show, but I ask you to imagine that the person giving the advice is very thoughtful and engaged in the conversations of their guests. One lady who had been in a relationship for ten years came on the show, and the guy had finally proposed. They were going to get married, and on their wedding day, all of her bridesmaids were prepared and ready. They were all getting their makeup done, and five o'clock rolled around, which was the time that the wedding was supposed to start (of course, we all know that no wedding starts on time), but no groom was there. So, the bride-to-be called her groom, and He said he was on the way. Six o'clock came around, no groom; seven o'clock came around, no groom; eight and nine o'clock came around, and the groom still was not there. His explanation for not being there yet was that he was stuck in traffic, and as time moved on, he said it was because his Uber had gotten a flat tire, but no matter what, no groom was there.

So, she sat there with tears in her eyes, and with her bridesmaid party all tearing up around her, she finally realized that she was not going to get married that day. In fact, the 10-year relationship that she had poured herself into and devoted herself to had come to an abrupt and painful halt. Now, where a new transition of life together was supposed to begin was the place she found out it ended.

As I sat there watching this show. I couldn't help but think how ten years of shared joy, pain, and love could go out the window. In a matter of hours, ten years of labor, devotion, trust, and fun times melted down into pieces into the ashes of what was and was no longer.

I could not help but think about some of the things that had happened to me. Although I've never been stood up at the altar, I have been stood up at the altar of my heart. I know what it is like to be rejected at a moment's notice. I know what it is like to be rejected by a friend who I confided in. I know what it was like to be rejected by a lover that I thought would be around for the end of time; I know what it is like to be rejected by family. I knew what it was even like to be rejected by mentors.

I thought to myself, "How can she learn to trust again?" and honestly, that is the point where I connected with the story the most.

For years, I went on, not knowing how in the world I could trust people again., after rejection.

You know, sometimes the rejection is the easy part; it's getting over the rejection that can be the monster. You see, the process generally goes something like this:

We look at what happened. We look at our part in the matter. We understand that something's happened, and every road has an end, and that sometimes people are just not very kind and don't know how to tell us the truth. Also, some people just don't see us as valuable enough to talk to us. So, then we get over that part, and precisely, that's what we've been doing through the journey in this book.

However, there is another part. After we have accepted what happened in a relationship and after we have taken responsibility for our part, and after we have looked at our wounds to the point where we are in a state where we can function, now we come to the hard part. The hard part has yet begun because after we've gone through everything, we still must know how to get up and try it again.

The people who I know live a lavish life by God's standards, not worldly standards; do not have the biggest house on the corner with the six-car garage and Porsches everywhere with Birkin bags galore. They do not have expensive trips to Paris or front-row seats at New York Fashion Week. They do not have millions of photographers trying to get the best picture of them to be posted on the front page of a magazine.

They have a life of freedom and serenity!

Every time I am around them, they have a peace that surpasses all understanding, a peace where they are free to move with God because they know that they are in good hands. They live with joy, and they lived as though they are free, not held back by the perceptions of others and what is going to happen. They live as though they know it is all going to be taken care of, and perhaps the most difficult part of the beautifying rejection experience is not getting over your rejection, but it's opening yourself up to love again, to trust again, to believe again, to know that you can have a healthy and full relationship again.

I must say, this is a journey that I am still on myself. After a divorce, many failed friendships, and relationships that I thought would last, it has all made me a little bit more careful about putting myself back out there in any capacity. Even as I write the words on this page, I would prefer not to take another risk or get my expectations up.

I think the hardest thing about believing again is taking a risk on if it may work out or how long it may take to get what you believe God for.

> *Hope deferred makes the heart sick, but a longing fulfilled is a tree of life.*
> Proverbs 13:12 *NIV*

Belief is a beautiful thing, but when we go through rejection, it taints us to not want to take another risk to love again. However, God has not given us the spirit of fear, and he does not want us to live in a perpetual state of anxiety, concerned about who will hurt us next and being controlled by that fear that causes us to not want to try again.

There is a song named "Run Wild" that I listen to by a popular contemporary Christian artist, Duo, named For King and Country. This one song of theirs stood out to me for perhaps six years or so. It stood out to me because that's what I saw in the people who I knew. God had recovered them and redeemed them from their rejection but even the more they were willing to take another risk!

Theirs a portion of the song that says:

"You're a lion full of power who forgot how to roar
You're an eagle full of beauty, but you can't seem to soar.
Will you return to the garden where we were first made whole? Will you turn to the one who can liberate your soul, Don't you want to Run wild, live free Love strong, you and me Run wild, live free Love strong"

BEAUTIFYING REJECTION: THE GREAT EXCHANGE

This song stood out to me at a time when I felt incredibly bound by life, depression, and rejection, so I would listen to it over and over because I knew that I wanted to live free.

Now the Lord is that Spirit: and where the Spirit of the Lord is, there is liberty.
2 Corinthians 3:17 *NIV*

The Bible says that wherever the spirit of the Lord is, then that means liberty is present because our Lord and Savior, Jesus Christ, is the actual Liberty we seek!

So, what is Liberty? It's freedom!

Freedom from rejection.
Freedom from guilt.
Freedom from shame.
Freedom from fear.
Freedom from regret.
Freedom from others' opinions of you.
Freedom to walk in power.
Freedom to walk in boldness.
Freedom to love.
Freedom to have joy.

Freedom to have peace.

You have access to all of these freedoms and more when you have Christ as your Lord because when you have Christ, you have his spirit, which is the embodiment of freedom. However, there is a caveat to truly living in freedom. It's being healed to the point where you're willing to try it again, willing to open yourself up and open your heart again!

When I discovered this truth, I understood it with my head, but my heart was screaming "absolutely not"! I'd always been taught that the definition of insanity was doing the same thing over and over again and expecting different results. I had forgiven others but the step of opening myself again shook me to my core. However, I wanted to *live free* and sometimes living free looks like being courageous in the places that scare us the most.

So, my thing was, if I was going to try again, what would be different this time than all the other times? The best way to get any answer is to go before the Father because surely God couldn't be so careless with my heart to put me back into danger. I wondered, "God, how in the world could you be asking me to open myself up yet again?", Not only that question but others like...

"What does it look like to open myself up again? How does this fit into the scripture that says "Guard Your Heart with All Diligence, for Out of the Heart Flows the Issues of Life, comes from the scripture of (Proverbs 4:23)? "

"How do you guard your heart when you love with people with your heart?"

"How do I enjoy relationships when I know that someone could potentially hurt me and reject me again?"

And my friend. I can't say that I've gotten all the answers to all those questions yet. I can't say that God told me that nobody would ever hurt me again, or that I wouldn't get mistreated, or I wouldn't be rejected again. I didn't get any of that. As a matter of fact, if I had gotten an answer, I probably wouldn't have even written this book, but I can say that God has made one thing very clear to me, and now I offer the same thing to you.

Living a free life has nothing to do with how or even what others will do around you, but it's about living a life where you lean on God and listen to his instruction as you love others. The purpose of everything in life is not to experience bliss away from rejection, pain, and heartbreak but rather to know that in an undependable and unpredictable world, we have a solid rock, that is our Kingdom Father, to run to when life has turned on us. It's about knowing that by following God, even if we go through a rough place, we can trust his plan when it requires us to take a hit (*take a hit was a reference from my dear sister, Minister Tiffany Amanetu).* For a moment, this may seem unfair, but living life like this is well worth the risk of potentially being rejected again because it's a Christ-centered life, not a Pain or Rejection-avoidance-life.

The enemy blows up rejection so big because he wants us to feel as though there's no cure for the pain that it brings into our lives. The real truth of the matter is that the enemy is scared that one day, we are going to trust God and let him lead us to kingdom connections regardless of what we have to go through. The enemy knows that one day our decision to move beyond our pain and rejection is going to give hope to someone who didn't have hope before. Make no mistake: the people you loved were a part of your ministry, and those who rejected you in your past were still changed and empowered by your love even though they hurt you. They still experienced the beauty and the love of God, through you, even though they did not know how to return it back to you.

> *"For God is not unrighteous to forget your work and labour of love, which ye have shewed toward his name, in that ye have ministered to the saints, and do minister." Hebrews 6:10 KJV*

Furthermore, the Bible says that God will not forget your labor of love. My aunt Lauria specifically called me one night after the Lord had put me on her heart. It was perfect timing, because I felt so low and beat down by life that I didn't know what up truly looked like anymore, and she said, "God said he will not forget your labor of love," and I nearly busted into tears. I had never paid attention to that verse before, but it truly connected to my spirit.

We never think about loving others in this manner, but honestly, loving with the love of Christ is labor; it is work. Our labor of love can be so overwhelming, and at times, it feels unfair. Sometimes, it feels like you can put so much time and effort into building, and it's as if it is too much to ask of your heart to give anything extra. This is why I believe rejection is so painful because when we sow our labors of love, in our human nature, we expect a return on our investment and if not received we feel devalued and used. Human nature and the basic principles of sowing and reaping says, "I invest in you, You invest in me," but in the Kingdom of God, that is not how it works (as my aunt Sheryl taught me).

> *" I planted the seed, Apollos watered it, but God has been making it grow. So neither the one who plants nor the one who waters is anything, but only God, who makes things grow. The one who plants and the one who waters have one purpose, and they will each be rewarded according to their own labor. For we are co-workers in God's service; you are God's field, God's building."*
> *1 Corinthians 3:6-9*

Allow me to metaphorically sit with you and hold your hand as I share this truth with you even though I myself didn't like it when I received it. The Bible says that one plants the seed and one waters the seed, but God adds the increase.

BEAUTIFYING REJECTION: THE GREAT EXCHANGE

Sometimes, the people who have been rejected the most are the people that God often sends to plant the seed of love into stony hearts. He uses the children he has in his kingdom who love hard and those who are willing givers to give to those who would potentially never seek God on their own, thereby never knowing his unconditional love. This means people like you and me become the forerunners of unconditional love to those of the world who can be deemed unlovable. We introduced the Kingdom gift of love in the lives of those who have never experienced it before.

I don't say this in a braggadocious way, but for example, I've come into contact with people who say, "I have never experienced someone who's so kind like you before". I'm sure that if you are reading this book that people have said that you're also so loving, or you're so open, or you're so willing to be a big help and assist them. That's because you actually do have a big heart, and oftentimes, the people who give the most generally are those who feel the most overlooked and misunderstood. After years of that happening to me, I just wanted to close shop and shut off the flow of my giving heart. Sure, I would forgive whoever overlooked or rejected me, but I just didn't want to give love and kindness away anymore because it seems that it was never appreciated. I wanted people to earn it, and while I do think there is something to be said for people earning your trust, I believe that no one can earn the love of God that flows through you!

When God brought up this thought about the lavish lifestyle, something about it radiated through me, my spirit, and my soul because to live lavishly is to know that the love you give is coming through you from God. This kind of love can't be purchased, or manipulated, or even hidden. The love of God is a stream that flows from within you that cannot be stopped up or shut off because it was created to flow lavishly on the earth and the people all around you, no matter the ROI (return on investment).

Even though pains, trials, and frustrations come through that same canal accompanied by the responsibility of loving other people and being open and willing to love again and experience life again and experience joy again, in relationships, the well of love still cannot be suppressed. We were created to love and to be loved by others, and the risk of love is necessary for our soul's survival.

BEAUTIFYING REJECTION: THE GREAT EXCHANGE

However, taking a risk and trying again does not mean that you are a sitting duck for the next blow of rejection. Living a lavish lifestyle is about knowing that there is a guarantee that makes all the difference in the world, and that is, we have our Father in Heaven to pick us up when we feel crushed by the winds of life and crushed by the rejection of life. That lavish love, and a lavish lifestyle do not depend on our perfection, our independence, and even more importantly, on man's perfection towards us. Having a lavish lifestyle is about continually opening ourselves up to the love of Christ that can be shared with everyone. It's about experiencing the beauty of a love that is so great that *"...He so loved the world that He gave His only begotten Son." (John 3:16)*

First, God so loved you and me that He lavished his love on us, and he spared no expense. The lavish life is about trusting that as we open ourselves up to the beauty of our future with the help of the Holy Spirit guiding us; We can live in the freedom of God to love people knowing that we have a blessed assurance in Jesus. We can be confident that we will not be forsaken by Him and that He will not leave us nor abandon us. Living a lavish lifestyle is about attaching our desires for love to God, continually attaching our choices, our freedom, and our peace to Jesus Christ, and being willing to constantly be open for love through him. When we open ourselves up to love through God, we can love men without the need for them to reciprocate it or to validate what we've given them. When we love like that, we're loving like God in full freedom, knowing that He will spare no expense for us, so we spare no expense to obey Him.

Welcome to your lavish lifestyle. Be free!

Prayer: *Father, I thank you for the gift of freedom; That in you I am free to live and love again. That rejection and the pain associated with it has no hold over me. Help me to remember that no matter what happens or what takes place in life, you are always my solid rock. In Jesus name. Amen.*

24

Reflect, Not Rebuke: Escaping the Trap of Judgment

> Judge not lest thou be judged.
> Matthew 7:1

The Bible tells us to examine ourselves, not judge ourselves.

A lot of times, when people have gone through rejection like you and I have, our guards tend to be on high alert. I can speak for myself when I say there was always a watchful eye for anybody who could potentially harm me with the pain of rejection or bring me back to that place of feeling powerless. I refuse to sit back in the seat of torment that is rejection, so I had to do everything I could in an effort to stop rejection before it even happened.

Out of this effort, I began to see and judge everyone as a threat; I considered everyone to be the same as the bullies of my past (which simply wasn't true). As a result, God had to call to my attention that I had begun to engage in judging people, not because I was evil, hateful, mean, or spiteful, but because I was scared.

I had been through so much with different friends and different groups of people that I had no belief that anyone was inherently good or that their words and what they said were actually the truth. So, I would constantly look at people and think they were judging me. I would think that somebody was always talking about me behind my back or judging me for my actions, which led me to live a life of defensiveness. Have you ever been in a cycle where you are constantly in the mode of defending yourself? That's exactly where I was.

I did this because I felt like my defensiveness and judgment of people and their actions would keep me from being judged and being in a vulnerable place again. However, a life of defense is miserable full of anxiety and speculation. I felt as though I was always on edge until God brought me to the place of healing. The Lord shared a revelation with me that initially sounded like a cop-out and excuse for other people's poor behavior. However, I came to realize that God's revelation was not just for them, but it was mainly for my anxiety-induced heart. Through revelation, I realized that I had to get to a mentally healthy state where I assumed that people were always just doing the best that they could, even when it was hard to believe.

The truth is that if we live in a perpetual state of defense, then we are essentially making the claim that we are responsible for our own protection, and while that may have some merit, it isn't entirely true.

The truth is that we are only defensive when we believe that someone else has the power to overcome us with their stance about us. So, in order to come out of defensive mode, we have to come to terms with the fact that no one's judgment or opinions of us changes a thing about God's love for us.

We must trust God that everything is still going to work out for our good, but that doesn't mean it feels good all the time. It all working out for our good just means that God orchestrate our life in our favor. We have to know that no one else's heart or mind is our responsibility, nor can it cause God to love us any less.

From people pleaser to God pleaser

As a recovering people pleaser, I realized that I had begun using the opinions of others (both good and bad) as my compass to navigate my life. I allowed the desire for others to like me to become the object of my affection. I could no longer live that way, and neither should you.

If I had continued to live in the mental space of living on the opinions, confirmations, and affirmations of men, then I would be swayed by their negative opinions of me too. One day, they would tell me that I was beautiful, and I would be happy, then the next day, they would tell me that my new dress didn't look good on me, and it would devastate me.

Reliance on men's words could keep us in a state of anxiety, constantly paying attention to their unsaid reactions to gauge their acceptance of us is a prison.

This way of living and thinking keeps us bound and constantly trying to protect ourselves from other people's words, but when we begin to attach our desires to God, then we have little need for Men's judgment (or our judgment of them). We must realize that our destinies are not attached to the judgment of Men or their opinions.

Now, I am not saying that this is easy to do because even as I write this, I acknowledge the hardship of going through judgment from people, especially the people we care about. On a very basic level, as human beings, no one wants to feel like others disapprove of them. It is our intrinsic desire to be a part of a group and to be accepted by them, but the truth of the matter is that while we are all human beings, we are all still made to be uniquely different.

"There is one body, but it has many parts. But all its many parts make up one body. It is the same with Christ. We were all baptized by one Holy Spirit. And so we are formed into one body. It didn't matter whether we were Jews or Gentiles, slaves or free people. We were all given the same Spirit to drink. So, the body is not made up of just one part. It has many parts. Suppose the foot says, "I am not a hand. So I don't

belong to the body." By saying this, it cannot stop being part of the body. And suppose the ear says, "I am not an eye. So I don't belong to the body." By saying this, it cannot stop being part of the body. If the whole body were an eye, how could it hear? If the whole body were an ear, how could it smell? God has placed each part in the body just as he wanted it to be. If all the parts were the same, how could there be a body? As it is, there are many parts. But there is only one body.

The eye can't say to the hand, "I don't need you!" The head can't say to the feet, "I don't need you!" "In fact, it is just the opposite. The parts of the body that seem to be weaker are the ones we can't do without. The parts that we think are less important we treat with special honor. The private parts aren't shown. But they are treated with special care. The parts that can be shown don't need special care. But God has put together all the parts of the body. And he has given more honor to the parts that didn't have any. In that way, the parts of the body will not take sides. All of them will take care of one another. If one part suffers, every part suffers with it. If one part is honored, every part shares in its joy. You are the body of Christ. Each one of you is a part of it."
1 Corinthians 12:12-27 NLT

The truth is that we are all made in God's image, but just because we're all made in God's image in one body and one baptism, that does not mean that every one of us reflects the same aspect of God, who is a multi-facet, God! I believe that when God made human beings, He put a little piece of himself into all of us that could only be reflected through each person in a certain way that He selected it to be showcased.

We reflect the differences of God.
  We reflect the personalities of God.
    We reflect the many attributes of God.

This is why we are the body of Christ because we're made up of many members within one body to do the work together.

There's not one fingerprint on this earth that is the same, maybe similar, but not the same, which is why it is important for us to acknowledge our differences and acknowledge that God has made us uniquely and beautifully. However, with that uniqueness, it can be a breeding ground for complex disagreements.

I grew up in a very conservative and traditional home with belief systems to match. At some points, Christian leaders made me aware that wearing pants, wearing makeup, and even women preaching was a sin. Of course, I've come to a place in my adulthood where I realized all of that was false.

However, after I got older and realized that all of that was wrong, of course, I was upset because I felt like I had been programmed incorrectly, which would ultimately send me on a long journey of purging and being retaught.

I honestly felt like someone had taken my time away from me, like someone had bamboozled me into believing that all of these things brought shame on me, damaging my self-confidence in adulthood. I will not lie; as a 21-year-old, this made me want to go off a little bit and confront a few people. Scorning me for wearing shorts (mind you that were down below my knees because my Mom and Grandmother didn't allow daisy dukes), and then others for wearing long fingernails and makeup, really put a damper on my exploration of beauty. This led to me becoming a young lady who constantly second guessed myself.

However, God made me realize that many of the Christian leaders did the best they could with what they knew at the time. They thought that abstaining from these things was their salvation and their sanctification. It wasn't their fault they had received a faulty, uninformed ideology. They were simply just trying to please God according to what they believed He wanted, just like you and me are trying to do today.

Searching for a better understanding, I thought about the people who created these rules and regulations for their church and denomination based on what they believed they heard. I then looked around the Christian community and realized one denomination believes one thing, and the denomination down the street believes another, not to mention the non-denominations that have their own beliefs and still function as denominations.

I then turned to my Christian friends, and one friend told me that God told them to do certain things. Then I had other friends who were also Christians, and God never told them any of that and yet told them something different. As a young lady, I thought to myself, "How could all of this be? How are we supposed to live our lives and please God if we all can't even agree? Who was in sin, and who was truly Holy?"

For a long time, I couldn't figure it out until I came to the revelation that sin really isn't rule-based; it's obedience-based. We sin when we are disobedient to the mandate that God has put on our life.

Sometimes, along the way of wanting to please God, we can tend to make certain things right and other things wrong. We don't always consider the fact that becoming who God wants us to be is not a cut-and-dry moment nor is it a white or black situation. God made us all different with different assignments and purposes coupled with personality traits that differ one from another, so with God, there is not always a one size fits.

If you look at the world around you, because everybody is given different marching orders by God, it can be very difficult for one to find His or Her way. As I was going through my own journey, it seemed like these things kept me bound for years because I thought I had to do everything everyone else was doing. These different things kept me confused between people pleasing, religious doctrines, and just always feeling shame, rejected, and left out; I felt like I just couldn't get it right, and after a while, I felt defeated and became bitter towards the people who seem like they had it all together.

In that place, my life had become all about getting a check mark from God and Christian leaders, but the problem with just trying to get check marks is that corrections seem like rejection. I became a harsh critic of myself, and the only thing I was receptive to was "good job," so if "work on it," was the critique, I would almost crucify myself mentally until I felt lower than dirt.

Finally, I came to a place where I just threw my hands up to God and said, "I can't do this anymore Lord...I cannot be this Little-Miss-Perfect-Good-girl. I try and try but keep messing up...".

Slowly, God began to open up my understanding to the fact that the only thing He's ever asked of me is to be obedient to Him and trust and believe Him, and He would be pleased.

He never asked me to please my friends or my Christian leaders.

He never asked me to be accepted into Christian groups (even though it is nice to be received).

He also never asked me to have all of the trinkets in the world. And He surely never asked me to be perfect.

He asked me to trust Him
He asked me to believe in Him.
He asked me to love others
He asked me to keep my eyes on Him
and be obedient to His word.

...AND HE would be pleased.

What I had to learn and what I hope to share with you is that there will always be somebody who believes (by their judgment) that the way you serve God and the way that you live your life is not correct or up to God's standards. I have also learned that these same people harshly judge because they've possibly created standards for themselves that have imprisoned them in a way that is not congruent with God's grace, which could cause them to possibly beat themselves up in private.

It's a trick of the enemy to make all of us strive in vain and expend our energy on proving that we are someone whom God has already confirmed and qualified us to be. Many do this out of the judgment of others, or even worst, the judgment of self.

Many may use the scripture of 2 Corinthians 13:5, which reads, "Test and evaluate yourselves to see whether you are in the faith and living your lives as [committed] believers. Examine yourselves...". *AMP*

However, the key word here is "examine" not judge. The word examine means to test or assess, and even in the original Greek word, peirazō(ref number G3984), it is congruent with words such as tempt, try, scrutinize, entice, and discipline. The very essence of judge or judgment is to come to the conclusion of a matter, but an examination is to evaluate the matter where it currently stands on its journey so that progress can be noted and observed for its future.

When we allow ourselves to fall into the judgment of others or even ourselves, we subject ourselves to conclusions and judgments that are inconclusive and inaccurate. Whenever we judge ourselves, we end a story that God still wants to develop within us, but it takes humility to examine ourselves and gratitude to be grateful for the ability to correct ourselves. Many times we try to judge ourselves because to judge ourselves or others says that we are in control, but to only examine says that we must pass it on to Father God, and He becomes the controller and higher authority, which requires another humbling.

> *"So then, let us [who minister] be regarded as servants of Christ and stewards (trustees, administrators) of the mysteries of God [that He chooses to reveal]. In this case, moreover, it is required [as essential and demanded] of stewards that one be found faithful and trustworthy. But [as for me personally] it matters very little to me that I may be judged by you or any human court [on this point]; in fact, I do not even judge myself. I am aware of nothing against myself and I feel blameless, but I am not by this acquitted [before God]. It is the Lord who judges me. So do not go on passing judgment before the appointed time, but wait until the Lord comes, for He will both bring to light the [secret] things that are hidden in darkness and disclose the motives of the hearts. Then each one's praise will come from God."*
> *1 Corinthians 4:1-5 AMP*

I believe we should strive to be like Paul who says, *"it matters very little to me that I may be judged by you or any human court [on this point]; in fact, I do not even judge myself. 4. I am aware of nothing against myself and I feel blameless, but I am not by this acquitted [before God]. It is the Lord who judges me."*

At this moment, I ask you to stop judging others and yourself.

The reason why many of us don't feel free and are weighed down is that we are sitting in God's judgment seat and trying to bare responsibilities that are not ours.

Judging others or even judging ourselves is not freedom or the lavish life that we are called to have.

Freedom in God starts when we get out of God's judgment seat and when we allow God to become our judge and Jesus our Lawyer.

What then shall we say to all these things? If God is for us, who can be [successful] against us? He who did not spare [even] His own Son, but gave Him up for us all, how will He not also, along with Him, graciously

give us all things? Who will bring any charge against God's elect (His chosen ones)? It is God who justifies us [declaring us blameless and putting us in a right relationship with Himself]. Who is the one who condemns us? Christ Jesus is the One who died [to pay our penalty], and more than that, who was raised [from the dead], and who is at the right hand of God interceding [with the Father] for us.
Romans 8:31-34 ASV

Freedom in life becomes obtainable when we begin to depend on God and trust His judgment more than we trust the judgment of other people and the judgment of ourselves. This is actually necessary to move into the freedom of the beautification process.

When you free yourself up from the need to get approval from others, it becomes easier to listen to their criticism and not become hurt, angry, or targeted. When God's word and judgment become THE STANDARD in our lives, other people's standards lose their effectiveness and power over us, and even our own reservations about ourselves have to bow in submission to the Fathers.

It is God who justifies us [declaring us blameless and putting us in a right relationship with Himself].

God justifies us, so therefore, His judgment is the most important judgment in our life. Our forever heart posture should be to ask God, "Are you pleased with me"? There is no one on this earth that can be pleased with you, that can justify or save your life, and since the ultimate goal of life is to receive salvation and serve God, then the one thing you want is for your efforts to go toward the pleasures of God. I would venture to say that as long as God is pleased with you, then nothing else or no one else judgment of you matters.

Prayer: *Lord, thank you for choosing me and justifying me to be in the right standing with you. I ask that you forgive me when I have made the judgment of people more important than the judgments of you. I thank you for the grace you have given me in the places of my ignorance. Remind me of who you are in my life when I forget that your judgments are more important than anything else. I pray that your judgments and your precepts be the measuring factor of my life from this day forward, in the name of Jesus. Amen.*

25

Crafted By The Divine: Living As God's Idea

Many times, out of being inspired and motivated by another person's testimony, we can get the impression that if we just do what they did, we can have what that person has. Our social media-driven world tends to be drenched in motivational messages that revolve around the idea that if one person can reach a certain height of success, everyone can reach the same height of success or greater.

There is no shortage of "Gurus" telling us how to create a list around habits, things we should do, and how we should look while carrying out various tasks associated with the success we desire. The desire to appear successful and being successful can sometimes lead many to create an image of success instead of walking out the actual process of what it means to be successful. However, if we zone in on the reason why many do what they do, such as stunting for Instagram and posting on tik tok, we can see that so many people are just as miserable as they would've been if they hadn't done anything, but they continue on in the falsehood of appearing successful because at least they "look" successful doing what they do.

To this point, it is no wonder why we have so many people who deal with depression, rejection issues, and feelings of inadequacy because we have set ourselves up to work while chasing the false pretenses of someone's Instagram success. It is easy for the desire to obtain the essence of those we admire to become our reasons for doing what we do. Some of us are on a hamster wheel running after a fake carrot, listening to endless motivational podcasts, and burning ourselves out in the process.

I, too, have been there where I was running after life with everything within me, only to end up in a place that looked nothing like what God had promised me. I was posting, doing the live videos, trying to dress a certain way and talk a certain way, because if those whom I looked up to became successful that way, I just knew I would have to take notes and implement.

However, nothing that I did worked, and yet I still knew that God had promised me that I would be successful just like everyone I looked up to, so what was I doing wrong?

Here's what I have learned from my experiences.

We can be meant to have the same thing as another person, but God will never do the same thing the same way.

We're not going to get it (whatever "it" is) by how we follow after another person, and we're certainly not going to get it by emulating their methods. Some things in life require a specified process that only heaven can create, implement, and monitor on your behalf, and the promises of God can never be toggled to appear by tips and tricks from our favorite gurus.

I have learned that the blessings of the Lord for our lives are always looking for the authentic version of who God is creating us to be through the beautification process. The promise literally comes looking for us along the path of beautification because God's specialized and tailor-made beautification process is our destiny's spiritual locator to find us.

The journey of beautification is the place where we decide to stand and surrender to God's truth of who God wants us to be and who we're created to be. It has nothing to do with whether we're posting on social media perfectly or even if we appear to be successful.

It has everything to do with us being open and surrendered to the place where God has called us to be, not looking to the left or the right to see who is doing what or how we can be like them.

The Rhythm of God in you

One of the biggest issues with working from someone else's model is that oftentimes, we see what they are doing but not the why behind it. This is very crucial because any strategist will tell you that the secret sauce is not in what you see, because "what" you see is simply just a byproduct of the bigger agenda. The "why" always exists before anything can appear because "the why" gives the instructions and direction to what needs to appear to bring the vision to life. However, when we are overzealous and so excited to make things happen, we tend to look at those who have accomplished what we desire and implement based on what we see without even questioning if that step will help us to get to our predestined place. We must realize that our lives and destiny operate in a special "why" that aligns with God's master plan. God's perfect plan creates a different rhythm for each soul on earth to operate by, and that is the promises of God yield fruit.

A huge part of beautification is learning your own rhythm in God and how you are called to dance in life to the beat that Heaven sets for you. When you choose to get into God's rhythm and realize that He alone is your dance partner, helping you to waltz through your greatest triumphs and deepest valleys, you will come to a place where operating and working from God's version of you is a part of your nature.

What's in front of you

> "…And let us run with perseverance the race marked out for us, fixing our eyes on Jesus, the pioneer and perfecter of faith. For the joy set before him, he endured the cross, scorning its shame, and sat down at the right hand of the throne of God. Consider him who endured such opposition from

sinners so that you will not grow weary and lose heart."

Hebrew 12: 1-3 *NIV*

As I talk about the rhythm of dancing and operating on Heaven's beat it may seem cumbersome. However, we must realize that God is not asking us to create a beat or dance. He is only asking for our commitment to listen and follow his lead. The dance floor and beats are already marked out for us, so all we must do is be willing to take our stance on the dance floor with Holy Spirit and let Him guide us.

Prayer: *Father, forgive me for the times I have chosen to dance to the tune of another person's beat. I pray that you help me to find my very own rhythm and pace that lines up with your will over my life. I submit myself to you, and I choose to focus on what is in front of me. Whenever I get off track and begin stumbling, looking at the fancy footwork of others, please help me to realign my vision with yours. In Jesus' name. Amen.*

www.ingramcontent.com/pod-product-compliance
Lightning Source LLC
Chambersburg PA
CBHW071656090426
42738CB00009B/1552